ForwardFast
Branding

The 6-Step Model to Accelerate Your Health, Science, & Technology Brand

Second Edition

BSB, llc
Boise, Idaho

Mark Stinson

I0465419

Praise for Mark Stinson

"When you engage Mark, be prepared to have fun, roll up your sleeves and get to work! His methods will draw out the collective knowledge and expertise of your teams. His StrategicGPS Navigation Process helped guide us from a few tens of millions to hundreds of millions of sales in the U.S. and worldwide. His multi-functional workshops in the process develop trust, create buy-in, and build accountability to assure success of the plan."

Dennis Burke, GM of Pharma & Medical Device Sales & Marketing

"Mark is a masterful facilitator and he has a broad cross-functional team (clinical to legal to marketing) to work together without barriers – to uncover a new view of the marketplace. In the end, the team was aligned (for the first time) and had established a logical and integrated short and long-term plan for the brand. It was magic."

Juli Cavnar, Strategic & Creative Marketing Agency Leader

"His book and a presentation are still fresh in my mind. As a member of the marketing team at MilliporeSigma, I have worked with Mark on many occasions and have attended his national and international presentations in Asia. His teachings helped improve sales in our Asia-Pacific markets. His style is very interactive and generates curiosity in mind of his audience."

Chandra Mohan, Senior Manager of Technical Marketing

"Mark and his team really had a solid process for how they would approach the advertising and communication challenges of our brand. I have recommended Mark to others by positioning him as someone with an immense creative mind, but who also can be very focused and purposeful. Mark is a diligent ally to have on your team and brings many impactful ideas to the table. Mark also has a number of useful processes to find information when a situation is murky, which is very common. I highly recommend Mark."

Dave Duff, Medical Communications Professional & Entrepreneur

"Mark brings a fresh perspective to all issues."

Mike Walsh, Business Development & Customer Relations Executive

"Mark was an incredible asset to support our growing company's branding and strategic efforts. He brought clear structure in the idea-to-action process, with a lot of communication and tracking toward execution and results Mark is a positive, active listener who can steer discussions toward the right direction. He is truly invested in his clients' success."

Elsa MacDonald, National Marketing Director

"Mark delivers Persuasion through Process. He is methodical in his approach, so he persuades people to understand his point of view in a very focused and yet, pleasant way. Writing needs discipline and ideas – he has both in plenty."

Rashmi Thosar, healthcare branding agency CEO

"Mark has developed a novel set of methodologies that can add value to any marketing initiative. Mark's approach is particularly effective in creatively capturing customer input in a way that helps ensure the input is both valid and relevant."

Art Morelli, Chief Business Officer & Pharma Leader

"I have great respect for Mark's knowledge, experience, and integrity for improving community health. He has a passion for an improved health system. He is a strong advocate and encourager of entrepreneurs to develop disruptive technologies and processes to improve the consumer healthcare experience and outcomes. Mark's leadership and consulting are focused on building collaborative relationships among healthcare entities that go beyond providing quality healthcare services and focus on health interventions that improve the quality of life."

Jim Giuffre, Healthcare Executive, Investor, & Consultant

"I met Mark in Brazil while he was facilitating physician qualitative research and we have partnered for a few years. His vast experience, his understanding of the healthcare market, and his innovative approaches have brought us the information and answers to the issues we need to move forward with the strategies needed to leverage our clients' businesses here at Brazil. One real benefit of working with Mark was getting to the heart of the matter of some issues that seemed to be very hard to solve."

Flavio Canelas, Chief Officer at Arteria Comunicação

"Mark is one of the most diverse and multifaceted businessmen that I have encountered. His ability to engage people at every level as I've worked with him in many capacities has gained my respect and admiration. Mark is a rare find, because he has the ability to get strong accountability, but not making you feel intimidated at the same time. I would recommend Mark to almost every group."

Jerry Henley, Marketing, Sales, & Capital Investment Executive

"The strategic process at most agencies looks like a black box. It can be frustrating for clients to work through this process with their agency because the process isn't clear and the results aren't always consistent. Working with Mark was a different experience altogether. I always appreciated the tools he developed and refined to bring clarity to the strategic process. They allow for everyone to speak a common language and ultimately lead to stronger collaborations."

Patrick Smith, Creative Director

"From my interactions with Mark, I find him to be delightfully curious and interested in understanding a problem from all perspectives. Anyone interested in an insightful and collaborative approach would find his way of thinking refreshing."

**Tammy Adams Spann, Vistage Chair &
Meeting Facilitator**

"Working with Mark has been fantastic. His leadership and facilitation at Confluence events created a stir and groundswell in the local innovation circles that we can do and grow and benefit the community more than we thought possible. Mark skillfully organized our discussion and helped us create new possibilities. I highly recommend Mark, his works, and his stewardship to any individual or company looking to draw out innovation and value."

Kaz Lawler, Innovation Technologist

"Our work together goes back more than a decade. During that time, I've come to value Mark's unique combination of talent, experience, expertise and sincere desire to collaborate with others as true partners. Mark's approach of active listening and mutual respect help elicit the clients' and my best strategic thinking. I observed his deft talent at presenting several great options in such a way that the client could easily and effectively "own" the process that resulted in world-class deliverables."

Jed Weiner, Healthcare Storyteller, Strategist, & Writer

"Mark has successfully put into practice this signature tool to help manage the complexity of the branding process by finding the intricate balance of all the brand attributes to maximize the effect. Mark's style in facilitating ForwardFast workshops is engaging and exceptionally insightful. ForwardFast is my go-to tool in providing leadership to clients to implement brand strategies for multichannel campaigns – from creative inception, market research validation, through to final tactical execution."

Pamela Boulware, Healthcare Marketer & Brand Strategist

"I have had the pleasure to work with Mark as a fellow member of the Idaho Technology Council's Tech2Market Committee. Mark has shown a gift for framing potentially complex issues in a way that is easier for the layperson to comprehend. I've appreciated his ability to organize the Tech2Market Committee. He has provided valuable structure to the committee's meetings as it moves forward to achieve its mission."

Paul Cooperrider, Technology Entrepreneur and Investor

"When it comes to brand strategy, there are plenty of authors and facilitators that talk a good game, but Mark Stinson helps you make it happen, and happen fast. I have watched Mark delight clients using the ForwardFast tool and have seen how effective it is in focusing the brand strategy."

Kathleen Pendlay, Senior Brand Designer

"Mark was great to collaborate with us due to his extensive, deep knowledge in the pharma industry – and a splendorous strategic way of thinking. I recommend Mark to anyone who's facing pharma marketing challenges, if you are looking for one of the best problem-solvers I've worked with. And somebody who does so through joy and lots of laughs."

Danilo Fratangelo, Agency Executive

Also by Mark Stinson

Books

- N-of-8: A Creative Group Innovation Model for Health, Science & Technology Brands

- Trusted Advisor Journal: Creative Inspiration for Elevating Your Consultative Relationships

- Wake Up and Live the Life You Love: Living in the Now (coauthor)

- Alone in My Universe (coauthor)

Innovation Classics

(Mark Stinson, editor)

- Notes on Nursing: What It Is and What It Is Not by Florence Nightingale

- Medical Essays: Homeopathy; Currents in Medical Science; Border Lines of Knowledge of Medical Science by Oliver Wendell Holmes Sr.

- Grappling With The Monster: Or, the Curse and the Cure of Strong Drink by Timothy Shay Arthur

ForwardFast Branding

The 6-Step Model to Accelerate Your Health, Science, & Technology Brand

Second Edition

Dedication

For Mom & Dad,

who made me the "brand"

I am today

Contents

PART III: APPLICATIONS

1. Corporate Brand

2. R&D and Manufacturing Process

3. New Product Introduction

4. Product Line Extensions

5. Interactive and Digital Branding

6. Services Branding

7. Clinical Trial and Scientific Nomenclature

8. Mode of Action Descriptions

9. Customer Experience Branding

10. Global Branding

11. Retail and Environmental Branding

12. Delivery System

13. Consumer Research and Insights Analysis

14. Package and Structural Design

15. Brand Evangelism

16. Conventions and Brand Events

17. Education Branding

Introduction

While there have been entire libraries written about branding, very few are specifically about branding for health, science, and technology.

It took me a long time to decide whether I should add another book on the subject. Would I be adding anything new to the literature? Would I be giving away proprietary secrets? Would I be writing myself out of a job?

But what I realized was that this information would indeed be helpful to people in the industry. It would help them understand that branding is a complex, living organism that needs tender care and gentle discipline.

Far from leading people away from me, this book might serve to draw them closer. We would be kindred spirits, on a quest to advance the art of branding in pharmaceuticals, diagnostics, medical devices, research technology, healthy foods, over-the-counter medicines, and integrated healthcare delivery.

ForwardFast is only a small part of what I do. It is but one of the tools in my toolbox. I think by elucidating on this particular tool, you could see that it's one that could help you, too. The purpose of this book is to tell a story because storytelling is a huge part of my day-to-day routine. Branding, on a certain level, is all about telling a tale, crafting characters and identities, and following a storyline.

Worried about the increasing number of people who love theories more than stories, filmmaker Ken Burns told the San Francisco Chronicle, "We are experiencing the death of the narrative. We are all so opinionated that we don't actually submit to narrative anymore. That's the essence of YouTube: Abbreviate everything into a digestible capsule that then becomes the conventional wisdom, which belies the experience of art." Stories are always more persuasive than opinions, which makes sense – wouldn't you rather someone delight you with tales of their experiences than listen to them recite dogma?

In the first part of this book, I'll discuss the principles of brand innovation. I will lay down some basic definitions so we can have a common vocabulary, and I will discuss some obstacles to the acceleration of a brand. I will also show you the impact of innovation – how branding will make a huge difference to your business.

In part two, I'll get into the work of the ForwardFast tool. In the first three chapters, I will talk about the basics of a brand. The next three will be a discussion of the possibilities. I will share references to books and companies that have principles I admire, as well as stories and case studies from my own past.

The third part of the book is all about applications of effective branding. It features a collection of examples you can apply in working with your own brands – with your own team of collaborators or with the agencies that work with your brands every day.

Throughout the book, I'll insert pieces of my own story as they pertain to the growing narrative of ForwardFast and the consultancy I built on the foundation of branding. A lot of this book presents universal information about branding, that might be applied in any market situation. However, all of this is designed around the particular profile of my firm – a health, science, and technology brand consultancy -- which as I will illustrate in more detail in Chapter 3, makes a difference in some specific branding challenges.

So sit back, buckle up, and hold on for the ride. This is going to go ForwardFast.

Addendum to Second Edition

Since its first publication, ForwardFast has become a go-to reference I share with brand managers who need a simple, direct visual foundation for branding — helping them to not only understand what the definitions really mean, but also how they relate to each other.

I have worked with creative groups from more than a hundred companies in health, science, and technology. I have written, supervised, and conducted hundreds of surveys, teleconferences, and focus groups for nearly every kind of pharmaceutical, device, instrument, and service imaginable. At last count, I have worked on more than 75 new product launches in my career. And my consultancy has created or advanced more than 200 brands since 2003. These brands range from Fortune 100 pharma corporations to start-up biotech companies, representing projects and research conducted in some 23 countries.

For sure, the term "second edition" suggests the book has been editorially revised and updated. The significance of the changes may be subjective, much like the way software publishers call one update "version 1.2" but label the next update "version 2.0." In some areas,

This second edition brings the model and the stories up to date, adding more recent case studies to illustrate the application of the model for managers who need to drive their brands forward. In some areas, I've added new and different content; in other places, I've simply modified the text slightly.

It also addresses questions that became even more relevant in the ensuing years — like questions about the impact of the financial crisis on brand investments and brand trust. I was interviewed on FOX Business News and was asked which industries and companies were branding the best in a weak economy. I told the host, Charles Payne, that "there is a temptation in this kind of economy and to hit the stop button on many of the marketing and branding efforts. But the companies that are going to come out on top when we come out of this are the ones that hit the forward fast button right now. The industries you see doing this are energy, finance, and technology. Another sector investing in improved brand experience is the service industries."

In updating the book, I pondered what we can learn from the past and what the future might hold.

Even as I was publishing the first edition of ForwardFast, there were key macro trends triggering industry change. These factors were impacting the basic assumptions of pharma brand strategies. In a limited-distribution report, a major global consulting group categorized these three trends:

- cost containment

- political environment, and

- increasingly complex healthcare infrastructure.

Certainly today, as we look towards the future, these challenges remain.

Price cuts are a leading cost-containment tool, and reference pricing has an increasingly important role. Biosimilar launches are set to improve cost containment in the biologics market. There is an increasing governmental role in promoting generics and biosimilars. The government is also promoting parallel importation. Healthcare provisions are continuing to be shaped by legislative and political events.

Layered on top of these macro trends are some internal industry developments.

The first is change to the R&D strategy that is helping to drive up productivity and increase commercialization of new products, particularly in the high-value biologics.

The second is increased globalization. This is in the context of the increasing impact of emerging markets on growth in the pharma industry. Emerging markets such as India, China, and Brazil have been lucrative to pharma and biotech players, giving them an ideal vantage point with which to develop and manufacture as well as provide expanded global customer and patient markets. This has given rise to rapid economic expansion, increasing healthcare spend, improved IP environment, and access to serve their huge populations.

Since the publication of ForwardFast, I've had the opportunity to travel to all three of these countries for client engagements. I have seen first-hand the impact – and potential – these emerging markets hold. I also have created strong partnerships and friendships with healthcare agencies and life science marketers in these countries. I enjoy having continued involvement with the successful brand strategies they are creating.

The third industry development is improved internal infrastructure that puts R&D closer to sales, marketing, and regulatory. To be sure, combined with continued industry consolidation and the increasing complexity of medical technology, brand development, and brand protection are key elements in driving and maintaining growth in the industry going forward.

When it comes to brand protection, it's amazing to look at the lengths companies go to protect their revenues involved in the brands. Since 2006, a range of strategies has been implemented by branded-drug companies to protect their products from generic and biosimilar.

For example, Zocor's patent expired in June of 2006. Merck implemented a never-before strategy to protect revenues of this blockbuster drug by entering into a deal with managed-care companies to keep Zocor on the cheapest tier of the insurers formulary. With generic simvastatin placed on the third and most expensive tier, this strategy was a significant blow for the generic manufacturers that had been granted 180-day exclusivity for the marketing of generic simvastatin.

Also in 2006, Pfizer discontinued its late-stage cholesterol-lowering drug torcetrapib. The company had invested nearly $1 billion in its development with the hope it would become available before the patent expiration of its leading cardiovascular drug Lipitor in 2010, thereby providing some brand portfolio protection. Another example is from Bristol-Myers Squibb and Sanofi-Aventis with their key blockbuster and market-leading anti-platelet agent Plavix, facing massive setback with an at-risk launch of a generic version of its drug by a Canadian firm.

Branded manufacturers also continually face attacks from counterfeit medicines which can overt sizable shares of brand revenues while also providing a significant threat to public health. The WHO announced that it would set up a global task force to fight this growing trade of counterfeit medicines which was subsequently implemented.

As I put all these macro trends and industry factors into perspective, writing this newly updated edition of ForwardFast helped make the model even more applicable to today's health, science, and technology marketers.

Overall, the intent of this book is to keep the model practical, relevant, and useful in the day-to-day efforts of branding professionals in pharmaceuticals, medical devices, diagnostics, research tools, and provider networks. Whether you work in a global healthcare corporation, a biotech corporation, a hospital products manufacturer, a drug delivery system developer, or a medical start-up, there are ideas here to move your brand forward... fast.

PART I:

THE ESSENTIALS OF BRAND INNOVATION

"Those who wish to develop and sell new products must locate the seeds of desire in the consumer and then nurture that desire."

Charles Bazerman,

The Languages of Edison's Light

Chapter 1:

A View of Branding from a Value-Added Perspective

Powerful brands lead to customer satisfaction. A clearly defined brand identity can aid customers' recall and can link a product to its qualities. A positive brand identity can make customers feel good about their purchase decisions, which leads to brand loyalty. Customers will allow that company to charge a premium price because someone loyal to a brand will expect to pay more for the quality product or service.

If powerful brands lead to happy customers, and happy customers buy your products and evangelize the brand to others, that translates into increased market share, higher stock prices, and increased future earnings.

Managing your brand innovation like you would any other company innovation – R&D, IP, patents, inventions, processes, etc. – just makes good business sense.

This outlook on branding can be traced back as far as Thomas Edison's brand of innovation. The world was changing for young Thomas Edison. Technology was making the world a different place, and someone had to make sense of it. As Edison grew and made a name for himself as an inventor, he found himself called to the field of electricity. Edison soon learned he had doubters. The challenge was one of marketing, and he rose to that challenge by creating a public presence: a definitive brand of innovation that made those who heard him pay attention. In fact, it was so uniformly accepted that Edison was on the verge of bringing electric lighting to the world that gas stockholders were on the verge of panic.

In 1882, he brought the system to New York City. The truly heroic task that Edison accomplished, though, had less to do with the specifics of his electricity and more to do with the way he created a mythology for the people – a lasting brand that resonates to the present day. He changed the world, not only in people's electrical capacity, but in their capacity to participate as a part of technology. He brought the elixir of light to the masses and made technology something familiar to all.

In the modern landscape of on-demand television, high-speed internet, technologically advanced business, and instant information, companies expect instant results. Everything is about speed. We want faster travel, faster-acting drugs, faster lines, faster computers, faster growth, and faster returns.

As an example from the pharmaceutical industry, consider Zomig Nasal Spray. If you're a migraine sufferer, the last thing you want to do is wait for a pain reliever to take effect. But you also don't want that effect to wane after just a few hours. What do you think migraine treatment is? What do you think fast is? Zomig throws both notions out the door – instead of a pill, it is a nasal spray for acute migraine treatment. And, instead of taking 2 hours to take effect, Zomig claims it can bring relief in just 10 minutes. This essential clinical profile for Zomig is central to its branding – they took the notion of a redefined drug and tied it into the brand character: a rocket-powered rabbit.

The goal of ForwardFast is to tap into the neurocircuitry of a brand. The speed of the mental connections in your brain is the metaphor on which I developed this process. That's how branding can pinpoint and penetrate the consumer's mind which leads to faster communication.

The ForwardFast model focuses on branding that will make people take a deeper look, generating a sense of wonderment. It can help you develop a great brand experience, one of quality and of memorability. And it can drive faster adoption of products, leading to bigger sales numbers at greater speed. These are the important factors of speed that move brands ForwardFast.

The value of branding is often forgotten until there is the question of who the brand belongs to. Take for instance, the value of the red cross symbol. In August of 2007, Johnson & Johnson sued the American Red Cross for trademark infringement. The two organizations share the red cross symbol, first claimed by J&J, under the agreement that the American Red Cross would not use the symbol in the commercial marketplace. In 2004, however, the American Red Cross started licensing the red cross to companies producing disaster relief products, some of which were in direct competition to products J&J makes.

So what was the real story behind this lawsuit?

As with anything that seemed so cut and dry, I chose to dig a little deeper. In the court of public opinion, the Red Cross won the battle. The entire situation was framed by the media as a greedy corporation putting the bottom line before humanitarian causes. However, the bottom line still goes back to trademark ownership. The symbol of the red cross was a trademark of J&J's since before the official charter of the American Red Cross. Despite that, the two companies have shared the symbol for over 100 years. Legally, J&J seemed to be in the right.

I can only imagine the discussions at both organizations since the settlement. In fact, J&J has continued to make charitable contributions to the American Red Cross, so while the relationship was certainly strained, it had not completely fallen apart.

The Big C Customer

One of the biggest keys to successful communication is to speak the right language to the right people. In branding, it is vital that this communication make an instant connection. Too many similar products are competing for attention. Your brand has to target a specific customer with a specific message that resonates with that customer. ForwardFast speeds communication by pinpointing the most important "Big C" customers and penetrating their perceptions with messages that lead to direct, and fast, action.

Your brand does not need to tell the potential customer everything about the product in one glance. That would be impossible, and if you tried, your brand would be a jumble.

Instead, your brand should entice a sense of intrigue about your product. You want to get your potential customer interested in learning more about your product. The trick is creating this sense of intrigue quickly.

Once you have a customer experiencing your brand, it is important that the experience is high quality. This may seem to extend beyond branding, but because brands are customer attitudes about a product, experience fits in perfectly. If your customers find your product difficult to use or understand, they will not buy it again and will not tell their friends to buy it. Developing this quality of experience from the very initial customer trials is vital to making future experiential gains.

In the world of medical product branding, experience is just as important.

For dermatological products, attributes that are associated with efficacy include touch, feel, and formulation. A fitting example from my own background is the skin care company that marketed Keri Lotion. Because Keri Lotion was a "skin specialist" brand with more emollient properties, it was perceived as more efficacious to the everyday store brand.

For a more complex market, neurologists using Botox for medical conditions (as opposed to cosmetic) found the experience of injecting Myobloc to be more difficult because dosing was not comparable to standard Botox treatments. But they found the experience of working with competent customer service and insurance support (and even sales reps) to be far superior. For that experience, a significant percentage chose Myobloc over traditional Botox treatments.

The ultimate goal is to create quick adoption. The faster people become loyal to your brand, the faster your sales numbers will pick up. All of this adds up to a faster financial return for our clients. It means economic value creation for the brand owner.

Value is provided by satisfying needs, but that is not the whole package. The key is to create a personality for your brand that is aesthetically pleasing and that tells the customer you stand behind your product 110%. I will show you how.

Speed is the thing. But that speed has to be more than just fast. It has to be quality. You have to be faster, better, and more efficient than your competitors. In the next chapter, I will discuss some of the differences that this speed requires, and in Chapter 3, some salient points on how to make your company move at the necessary pace. It is important to understand, though, that branding today is about fast response:

- Speed of communication

- Speed of intrigue

- Speed of experience

- Speed of adoption

All of this leads to speed of financial return. If you can deliver this speed, you are on your way ForwardFast.

Chapter 2:

"Play" versus ForwardFast

In the last chapter, we looked at the speed of the industry. This chapter discusses how to make that speed happen. As a writer, I am a big proponent of metaphors, so I use one to describe the difference between a basic brand and a successful one.

The metaphor is a remote control.

And the difference is one of "Play" and ForwardFast. In this chapter, I will describe how this difference is relevant. "Play" is science; it is the tried and true, testable, and safe method of branding. ForwardFast is more like art; the manipulation of sensory and emotional experience on all levels. This distinction is vital to understanding the ForwardFast model.

Let's take a look at the Forward Fast model – what it is, what it does, when to use it, how it's different, why that difference is meaningful to consumers and why this difference is relevant to marketing teams.

What is ForwardFast?

A 6-step model for defining brand attributes. The 6 brand attributes are:

- Likability
- Logo/identity
- Quality offering
- Brand associations
- Brand attitude
- Quality experience.

What does ForwardFast do? It documents and aligns the team on the strategies and tactics of the brand.

When is ForwardFast used? When organizing customer insights, writing creative briefs, developing tactical plans, identifying and filling gaps.

How ForwardFast is different: More than just a logo, packaging or materials, it's a total view of the brand as a product and experience.

Why is that difference meaningful to healthcare customers? It creates cohesive and consistent engagement with the brand. It fits into their world to improve it, not disrupt or interrupt it.

Why is that difference relevant to marketers? It provides a comprehensive blueprint for evaluating designs, programs, campaigns, processes, thought leaders, studies, support and even hiring salespeople and pitching investors.

A lot of intelligent people have done a lot of work to figure out the recipe for successful marketing. These methods have become the best practices - proven, basic ways to write copy, produce layouts, and develop messages and visuals. The idea behind these methods, the science of marketing, is to follow the recipe. Use the prescribed ingredients. Don't just rely on what you think.

There is good thought to this method. Why reinvent the wheel when you don't need to? I'm not suggesting anyone throw out their Play button – but I am suggesting that exceptional branding is about more than just "Play."

And that is where ForwardFast comes in. As we discussed in Chapter 1, people want things fast. Businesses, especially technologically savvy ones, want instant results. This is driven not only by technology, but also by three additional factors:

- Consumers demand constant innovation

- The service bar continues to be raised

- Investors expect to earn their return faster

We must innovate beyond traditional thinking. We must think beyond the safe boundaries of branding science and move into the realm of art.

"Play" is somewhat sensory. It certainly taps into visual recognition with layouts and graphics, and may move into the realm of auditory when considering jingles and commercial sound. But ForwardFast is full 5-D sensory. It takes into account all the senses – not only how a logo looks and sounds, but how it feels, smells, tastes. And it takes into account the emotional gut reaction to a brand. When you take a ForwardFast perspective, you are bringing in the full sensory experience.

- **Visual:** Layouts, graphics

- **Auditory:** Jingles, sounds

- **Olfactory:** Fragrance, scents

- **Tactile:** Texture, feel, touch

- **Taste:** Flavor, texture, mouthfeel, smell, sweetness, spice

The ForwardFast model guided my team's involvement in the brand development and launch for Berinert, a plasma-derived drug for a rare disease called hereditary angioedema (HAE). My work with the drug, or more specifically, with branding the drug, began in 2005 when CSL Behring engaged us to help develop the brand message for Berinert. This led to the development of the award-winning AllaboutHAE.com disease awareness print and web-based educational branding. In the last half of 2008, the team moved into the next phase of Berinert brand development – global hallmarks. To ensure a worldwide perspective throughout the process, I collaborated with a global network of partners from an RFP process right through to launch. This network tapped into diverse agency talent to generate initial thinking, drive discussion, and gain insights. Along the way, I worked closely with the client and more than a dozen country marketing managers to refine the brief and advance the global strategy. But before our visual identity group began its exploration – through extensive color and typography audits, creating a design framework – we used the N-of-8 process to create a strong foundational story. Our main objectives for story development were to ensure that all developed materials were on-target and persuasive to physicians and patients, to create compelling messages that connected directly with the customers, to convey CSL Behring total brand value proposition, and to evaluate creative concepts and promotional pieces to identify areas for needed refinement in telling the story in multiple media.

That was the starting point.

At the completion of the process, the team engaged a wide variety of design audits and design studies to uncover trends and identify opportunities for visual branding. The logo, logotype, and colors were developed for the Berinert branding to better tell the story of speed. In addition, the N-of-8 process channeled our verbal brand team in writing a clinical monograph, a product highlights brochure, and the brand standards guidelines book. Finally, my agency executed market-specific brand launch campaigns including sales materials, patient literature, support programs, and journal advertising. Together, these elements worked together to tell the Berinert story consistently in verbal, visual, and scientific terms. Ultimately, a global brand was forged.

What does your brand sound like?

Branding is about a lot of things — storytelling, connection, memorability, experience. Most medical and technology brands focus on making some pretty basic connections, but one that often takes the backseat to visuals is sound. DMI Music and Media Solutions has been thinking about sound for years. Their philosophy is simple: the best way to create loyalty is through emotion, and the best way to create emotion is through music.

My idea stretches from that. In creative brainstorming sessions, I've often applied an audio element to the workshop. I might bring in 20 sounds that reflect the business and see how they resonate. The group thinks about the product and figures out what sounds come to mind first.

During a recent branding assignment, I had an opportunity to apply the concept of audio branding. When designing the campaign (which included a website, video, and interactive training CD) the design team developed the characteristics of the logo – then added a custom-designed sound effect that incorporated the qualities of the brand.

A myriad of companies have used sounds to great effect. Sprint was so clear you could hear a pin drop. And who can forget the signature sound of Intel Inside? This becomes especially useful in the modern landscape. With the advent of phone ringtones, you can provide your brand sound for free download.

Sound is everywhere. Let's tap into its possibilities.

In concluding this chapter, you can see that both Play and ForwardFast are essential to successful branding. You must move things forward using both science and art in order to be successful. Play is not enough. So you have to make ForwardFast work. In the next chapter, I will look at how to make that happen.

Chapter 3:

Applying Brand Innovation

Who is your "Big C" customer? By that I mean who is your most important customer, the one you would spell with a capital "C"? In other words, who is the most important member of your audience? This is possibly the most important question to answer, and it makes a difference in branding efforts from the start. Why? It goes back to communication. Face time with customers is so expensive these days. It is difficult to get in front of the audience, to really get them to hear your message. It is key to know who you need to speak to and what you need to say to them.

What happens when you re-think your "Big C" Customer? Coca-Cola made a bold marketing shift under the leadership of then-marketing chief Joseph Tripodi. The shift was based on the hypothesis that the most important customer is the big retail outlet, not the individual consumer. They switched their "Big C" Customer from an individual to stores since most beverage decisions are made on the spot in-store. Take a page from Coca-Cola and focus on the "Big C" Customer – the one who can best help. And consider the right channel, too, not just the right customer.

My own consulting experience illustrates how to apply the strategy. As I mentioned in the introduction, my focus is on a very specific niche audience – health, science, and technology products, including pharmaceuticals, diagnostics, and devices. For these brands, the audiences are generally medical and life science professionals, though they can be further segmented into "Big C" customer groups.

Cardiologists, for example, are much more data-driven than other doctors. They specialize in the heart and cardiovascular system and, as such, focus on keeping the pump working and the pipes clear. Their primary consideration is the overall health of the patient but they direct their attention to the systems they specialize in even more. When branding drugs to be used by cardiologists, it is important to take this perspective into account.

Two drug brands I've worked on illustrate this point: Coumadin and Exanta.

Coumadin was a well-established therapy but the treatment was challenging for physicians to manage and for patients to comply. The branding and communications materials were developed to help these customers overcome the challenges of this drug. Even the colors of the various tablet strengths were part of the brand. Rather than downplay the complexity, the marketing strategy was to acknowledge it and help doctors make Coumadin practical to use. The communications campaign embraced the challenge, knowing that the "Big C" customer cardiologists' would find their mastery of Coumadin to be appealing.

Exanta is a completely different story. Its initial promise of innovation was to make life easier by eliminating the complex monitoring required for Coumadin. Because of the psychographics of cardiologists as experts in monitoring the whole system, they didn't necessarily want something easier. In essence, the feature may have marginalized the expertise of the doctors. In addition, because cardiologists demanded so much data, large-scale clinical trials of Exanta were conducted. These studies eventually exposed an intrinsic side effect that no one thought existed, which is why it was never approved by the FDA.

The big difference this regulatory environment poses, especially when connected with the fast-moving philosophy I espouse, is that a cross-functional team is necessary. Many team members will be involved in all aspects of product design, so everyone needs to be able to pull weight on the project. It requires a small cadre of versatile performers who know how to run, multi-task, and stay positive and energetic. No walking or moping allowed in my office. This also means that one of my most important jobs is to keep the energy level up in the office.

The best way for me to explain this is by comparing and contrasting "normal" marketing with the branding for science, health, and technology.

What universal branding rules apply and what additional rules do you have to apply when branding a specialized product?

There are many specific differences that exist for the branding I do. First, there are official regulations that need to be followed. Second, health claims have to be made carefully. We cannot over-promise about health improvements. Third, the process requires a good deal of scientific rigor. And finally, there is a broad range of team effort at all levels of production. All of this makes the branding process that much more intense.

The FDA imposes exacting requirements, regulations, and restrictions on all aspects of medical communication. Keeping up with all of these regulations can be a full-time job. And it can be an expensive business. For example, new drugs must have their name submitted to the FDA for approval. Industry experience shows that fewer than one-third of proposed names are approved. So, for a vast majority of the names, the entire naming process has to be started over again.

This is not peddling snake oil. One cannot make claims that drugs are going to do something they are not going to do. So it is important to have a good understanding of the science and clinical trials behind the product. The ForwardFast model helps make sure that the drug brands get a true, clinical, and scientific examination. This means gathering references and support for any claims.

Perhaps the trickiest aspect to all of this is the sheer number of stakeholders that are involved. It means that you must create a consistent brand experience across many audiences. It must appeal to all decision makers – it must come together for the entire group. Think about the sequence as a drug progresses:

- The drug company markets the drug

- A doctor specifies the drug

- A pharmacist dispenses the drug

- An insurance company pays for the drug

- A patient administers the drug (in most cases).

The brand team must come up with a strategy that takes all of that into account.

Who is your audience? That is what this chapter has been about. Branding is about tailoring an identity with a specific target in mind. In order to really make an impact with your brand, start by knowing your audience – really knowing who your Customer is.

In the next chapter, I will look at some of the obstacles to acceleration.

Chapter 4:

Overcoming Obstacles to Acceleration

In the pharmaceutical industry, drug advertisements are required to show "fair balance" – this is the fine print section of an ad that lists side effects, warnings, precautions, etc. Given that I am in the business of marketing pharmaceuticals, I thought I would include a "fair balance" section to this branding model. Anyone can use ForwardFast as a "how-to" manual, but it is more than a checklist for you to tick off as you complete your branding. As I have stressed, this is as much an art as it is a science.

As discussed in the last chapter, one of the keys to making ForwardFast work is a focused, cross-functional team. Because of that, there are some inherent risks involved, which are related to the difficulties in engaging a full team and the in-team dysfunctions that arise. Also involved is the notion that simultaneous execution/implementation is impossible. There are also some smaller speed bumps that arise that I will discuss. And finally, there is the notion of timing and luck. These elements must all be in balance for a successful execution of this model, which is a lot to juggle.

Of primary importance is a well-functioning team. Many books and resources exist for forging effective teams, including Lencioni's Five Dysfunctions of a Team. He shares a series of pitfalls that teams typically run into. Each one builds on the next, and if you are not careful, the entire enterprise can fall apart or be so dysfunctional it might as well fall apart. I prefer to switch this around, and observe things from the opposite perspective – how each of these aspects can be applied to build a better team. Using Lencioni's words, a team needs Trust, Conflict, Commitment, Accountability, and Attention to Results.

1. Trust

Trust is the ability to feel comfortable with vulnerability among team members. Innovation comes from openness, and I strive to make my people feel free to make mistakes, show weaknesses, admit to skill deficiencies and interpersonal shortcomings, and ask for help.

What happens in a team that shares trust is that, instead of focusing on strategic defensiveness, they work together to get the job done. Time is better spent, meetings are more productive, and morale is higher. The key to making this work is a culture of trust in the workspace, and that begins with yours truly setting the tone and the example. I have to be willing to admit to mistakes in front of the team, and I cannot punish team members for exhibiting vulnerability.

2. Conflict

Productive conflict helps teams grow. For conflict to be productive, it must be centered around concepts and ideas rather than on personal issues. This kind of conflict helps a team work out ideas for the best result. In branding business, this should be easy – everyone on the team should know that brand tastes differ – but often there is a tendency to focus on speaking for one's self, instead of the customer (doctor, patient, payor, etc.). Passion and emotion play a huge role in conflict, and in the discussion of how best to proceed, I strive to make team members feel comfortable sharing their true opinions. However, just because there is emotion involved, there should not be a feeling of anger at the end of the debate. The benefit to productive conflict is that it gets the issues out on the table and solved, rather than letting them linger and crop up again and again throughout the life of a project. Again, I see it as my role to promote productive conflict – first I model the proper behavior by not avoiding conflict when it arises; then I also allow team members to work out their own conflicts among themselves. If I constantly act as peacekeeper, no one wins.

One of the best examples of productive conflict is work with co-marketing partners. In a typical co-marketing arrangement, one big company and one small company work together on the branding effort of a major product. Sometimes these two companies will have conflicting goals. But I've found that creating a strong brand purpose and brand platform helps everyone work together on common strategy. With this foundation, the partners can more productively work through their differences.

3. Commitment

Effective teams are committed to the group goals and to the customers' benefit. In the health industry, there is an additional commitment to good health. Decisions of effective teams are made succinctly and clearly, and even those who voted against the chosen course of action go along with the decision because they know their opposition has been heard and considered. Effective teams move forward on a decision without any uncertainty that it will work because they know that the team will work together to make it happen – that is commitment to the goals. Team members act decisively and work effectively toward the goals the team sets. In order to promote commitment on my team, I encourage them to take calculated risks. Every day, I push teams to stay on target to schedules and event plans. I also strive not to place too much value on certainty or consensus.

4. Accountability

Accountability means the ability and willingness of team members to call their peers on their mistakes (and, going back to trust, the team members will be willing to admit their mistakes, so this should not be a problem). The key here is not about assessing blame or figuring out where "the buck stops," but for the team members to exercise peer pressure to keep the team on target. I encourage my team to self-manage, but I also keep them accountable using data, metrics, and timelines. In addition, I am willing to point out team responsibility when the team fails. A results-focused team knows what the benchmarks are for success, and they constantly pay attention to where the team stands in relation to those benchmarks. Financial results and status need to be secondary to goal-oriented performance. Paying too much attention to the bottom line or to where the team or individual stands in the eyes of the group is a clear means to failure. Instead, team members should focus on improving the quality of the brand experience. Again, in my case, I have to set the tone, objectively evaluating teams and individuals based on results and giving out rewards based solely on performance.

Another potential roadblock small teams bring is that simultaneous implementation may be impossible. You can't wait until everything is perfect or even complete in this model. So you must develop a staged rollout. This creates a dangerous "running with scissors" condition. Too many components are on the edge of failure. Employees feel like they are one step away from eventual doom. It can be rough on morale if you are not careful. What it takes is planning, calm, and a great team.

The nice thing about these factors of effective teams is that they build on each other. You can start with trust, developing that openness to being vulnerable. People who are open with their feelings are able to engage in productive conflict about issues and projects. Those teams that bring up their conflict issues are more able to be committed to outcomes, even if they disagree with the final decision. Committed team members are going to hold each other accountable for team success, and if they have trust and are comfortable with conflict, they will be able to call their peers on failures.

5. Attention to Results

Finally, if all of the above are in place, the team will be focused on results. Each member of the team has a stake in the outcome, and each person feels they have had a hand in the outcome. Successes can be celebrated together, and failures can be learning experiences.

Beyond the five dysfunctions that Lencioni describes, there is one is personal frustration of mine: The "W" word, Waiting. It makes the hair on the back of my neck stand up. Wasting is more like it. I banned the use of the "W" word in my office. It is kind of a tongue-in-cheek way of clarifying the attitude I want employees to have. Waiting implies passivity. "I'm waiting for them to call me back," "I'm waiting to get a meeting," "I'm waiting to get approval." It is passive. It is reactive. It is a waste of time. What I want to elicit with this word ban is an attitude of proactivity. Instead of waiting for them to call you back, plan in advance the time when they are scheduled to call you back. Instead of waiting to get a meeting, take the meeting to them. Instead of waiting for approval, schedule a review meeting. It is about controlling the action and planning for the future, rather than letting things fall where they may. No more waiting.

In any business, there are speed bumps – little things that don't necessarily stop progress but that prevent going ForwardFast. The design business is no different. Four of these speed bumps stand out to me as pretty basic items that continue to crop up time and again: quality, product failure, regulatory issues, and contract suppliers. Each has its own unique characteristics and brings its own concerns. But each can also be anticipated and planned for.

The first is quality. It is difficult to produce quality work day in and day out. There are bound to be little mistakes here and there, and as the projects move down the chain, these small quality issues can add up to big ones. With care not to bottleneck projects, quality control is vital at all stages. It will save you a lot of egg on the face down the road.

Less common, but still a concern, is product failure. Because I work with cutting-edge, still-being-tested pharmaceutical and medical products, there is always the chance that the product will end up not working. The key to dealing with this type of situation is strong relationships. Most companies don't have just one product, so doing a great job and making great contacts may secure you future product assignments. No one has a crystal ball – sometimes products just don't work out. But positioning yourself at all times to develop relationships can keep you from getting slowed down too much by this speed bump.

Always a danger, regulatory issues loom large. The FDA holds up products more often than anyone would like. But it happens, so how can you prepare? First, knowing the most common areas likely to produce regulatory issues is important for planning. You want to be sure to leave extra time for these items. Second, designating experts on your staff who have a stake in the compliance of what is submitted. Regulation information is readily available, and it sometimes takes a full-time employee to be up-to-speed on what is in and what is out.

Whenever you rely on people outside your organization, you chance difficulties. Problems with contract suppliers are the most common example of this type of speed bump. Again, the key here is relationships. It takes some time to develop, but you must build relationships that are mutually beneficial. In a pinch, the suppliers with whom you have good relationships are going to be more willing to help you out. The key is to make personal connections with individuals. They are much more likely to be there for you when you need them. And remember to thank those individuals appropriately when they provide their assistance.

Though there are plenty of areas to run astray, with some forethought, it is not too difficult to avoid most of the problems. Remember, the key to this model is speed, so you want to avoid as many detractors to that speed as possible.

Timing is something you plan for; luck is something you hope for. My attitude is that if you get lucky, it's gravy. But you can't count on it. And you shouldn't. So you're left with timing. For anything we do the timing has to be right. Studios launch new movies on specific dates. Do you think that is by chance? Will Smith has had some of the top-grossing movies of all time, and for a decade he released on July 4th weekend. Coincidence? I don't think so.

Timing comes down to two factors: seasonality and environmental factors. "Seasonality" refers to taking the buying season for a particular product into account when you plan your launch. Environmental factors are related to seasonality – they are the specific factors that change based on the seasons.

When I was marketing PreSun sunscreen, the client's objective was to get dermatologists' recommendations in February. By Spring Break, the buying season for sunscreen is over (how many bottles of sunscreen do you buy in a given year?). This same mentality is what drives retail stores to put up holiday displays early – after a certain time frame, folks are already thinking about the next holiday.

Environmental factors are something where counter-intuitive logic can get you somewhere. The conventional wisdom is that summer is the worst time to try to make sales visits to doctors' offices: the doctors are on vacation and the offices are less busy during these times. But the fact that other sales reps are not selling gives you a competitive advantage, and the slower business might mean the decision makers have more time to let you pitch your offers.

Related to seasonality is the annual scheduling of key congresses and conferences. It is essential, for example, to know when and where major conventions are held (such as those of the American Heart Association, American Academy of Allergy Asthma and Immunology, American College of Rheumatology, and the Radiological Society of North America) in areas associated with the product you are branding.

Being aware of product seasonality and environmental factors, then, becomes incredibly important to getting your message heard. There is no point in sending your message if no one is on the other end to receive it.

Moving ForwardFast is fraught with threats and obstacles. It requires a tight, effective team that is cross-functional and able to work at running speeds. There are pitfalls to any team's integrity, but the role of the team is so enhanced in my model that managing that team becomes intrinsic to success. Also vital is the ability to plan ahead and to stage rollouts of design products. Speed bumps are inevitable, and it is important to know how to anticipate and navigate them. Finally, there is the notion of timing and luck, both of which have a close relationship with how well your implementation works.

In the next chapter, I will explore the impact of using the ForwardFast model. It explains the specifics about how this model can benefit you and your operation.

Chapter 5:

The Impact of Brand Innovation

The ForwardFast model is all about achieving more with fewer resources. Efficiency is the name of the game. In the previous four chapters, we have explored the basic concept of branding as a value-adding proposition, the difference between "Play" and ForwardFast, how to apply brand innovation, and a few of the obstacles to acceleration. In this chapter, I discuss how using the ForwardFast model can change the way you do business. First, I will look at how it impacts media decisions. Second, I will show you how a ForwardFast focus can increase your return on investment. Finally, I will discuss the impact that using this model has on future innovations. Overall, this chapter will sum up the first section of the book, showing you the completed picture of the ForwardFast model.

Reach and frequency are talked about a lot in media purchasing. What kind of audience does the media reach? What is the frequency of the publication? Those are key factors in normal "Play" marketing, and they are good questions to ask. But in ForwardFast thinking, the goal is to speak succinctly to the right people. Remember that it is better to whisper in the right ear than to scream your message across a crowded room.

A great brand speaks to the right people. You will reach more people with less frequency. And if you are targeting the right audience, you don't have to reach as many people. As your message grows, word of mouth (the evangelist effect) takes over.

In Part II, I will discuss the elements of a great brand in more detail. For now, the basic point is that a great brand connects to people in a profound way. The key is to figure out who you are trying to connect to before you try to build that brand connection. Until you identify that audience, your brand cannot have impact, or if it does it will be random, sporadic, and will not compel your audience to do the talking for you.

When you know who your audience is, what they like, what they care about, how they think, then you can target your communication to them. You don't have to communicate as often or reach as many people if the things you are saying speak to the values of the right people.

Often the brands with the most impact say the least. Have you ever seen an innovative product that had great design but failed? These products were heavily invested in the wrong places. Without a great brand, without a compelling story that touches people, without a commitment to the user experience, there is no return on the investment.

There are simply too many products out there that compete with yours. It doesn't matter what your product is. Most consumers are savvy to this – they recognize that products are largely alike. One ibuprofen tablet is like any other. The key is creating a brand identity. Why would a customer want to buy Advil over Nuprin or the generic brand? Instead of being "Little. Yellow. Different," Advil is "the every pain reliever." You should not accentuate that your product is different, you should explain how it is different.

ForwardFast also has an impact on a company's ability to further innovate. One great innovation leads to another. As a company learns what it is like to be successful, employees will take on the innovative spirit. Innovative talent will be attracted as the reputation of the company grows. Suppliers will want to work with the company, to be a part of what that company is doing. When the public sees a company as an innovator, customers will look to the company for the next big thing and the press will further the story. Think of Apple. Everything they touch is touted as The Next Big Thing. Their past success is now their reputation. However, it is not okay to rest on your laurels – despite numerous successes, all it takes is one failure to blemish your brand image as an innovator.

The impact of ongoing focus on innovation is documented by rigorous business analysis. In 2009, Datamonitor looked at the performance in potential of 10 different sectors of the healthcare landscape ranging from medical diagnostics and devices to over-the-counter drugs to prescription benefit management and animal health. It concluded that prescription brands had the greatest potential as measured by market size times the average operating margin. Because of this potential, it recommended that pharma-focused companies should maintain their focus.

Conversely, those companies that drifted or over-diversified away from branded pharmaceutical sector could suffer performance dilution. Pharma companies should, therefore, endeavor to capture growth from emerging markets and high-value biologic therapies in addition to synergies from consolidation and mergers and acquisitions within the branded pharma sector.

Looking back, this impact has been proven among major companies which have pursued this strategy.

To take this insight even further, maintaining a focus on innovative branded products means blunting the impact of generic and biosimilar products. In my consulting with clients over the years, I helped create brand innovation strategies that explored many angles:

1. New Delivery Systems for dosing convenience and compliance or, even better, for reduced side effects.

2. Contracting & Collaborative Arrangements with Plans/Payers, with added services for formulary access and/or preference

3. More Clinical Studies to keep high-writers engaged with the brand for new indications

4. Leverage Patient/Consumer preference & demand

5. Provide specific direction on how to properly write the prescription to make sure patients get the branded product

6. Leverage HCP Positive Experience, Trust and Confidence in the branded molecules

7. "Narrow Therapeutic Index" or NTI

8. Co-Branding

9. Promote Support of Future Breakthroughs

In summary, the ForwardFast model can provide structure, strategy, and direction for greater marketing efficiency. Now that I have established the basic concept of how a brand creates value, you can apply the differences between "Play" and ForwardFast.

PART II:

PUTTING BRAND INNOVATION TO WORK

"Purveyors of new technologies must make hopes seem realizable, project anticipated but unproved benefits, promise plausible but uncertain long-term costs, and elevate their future systems above current real options to entice risk-taking customers to buy into the dream so as to make the dream real."

Charles Bazerman,

The Languages of Edison's Light

To review, Part I of this book illustrated the power of branding. Chapter 1 looked at the value branding can add to your organization. You learned that powerful brands lead to customer recall, brand loyalty, and, ultimately, premium prices. Chapter 2 taught us that traditional marketing techniques are good but that the ForwardFast model can accelerate your brand's success. Next, in Chapter 3, I talked about how to apply brand innovation. I told you about the notion of the "Big C" customer – as I explained, it is all about talking to the right customer. Chapter 4 was the "fair balance" section – it was all about the obstacles to acceleration that come with branding for the science and technology market. Finally, in Chapter 5, I examined the impact that the ForwardFast model can have on your company's media decisions, return on investment, and future successes. Great branding is a powerful tool that can dramatically improve your business.

Let's consider a classic definition of a brand. A brand is the symbolic embodiment of all the information connected with a company, product, or service. A brand typically includes a name, logo and other visual elements such as images or symbols. It also encompasses a set of expectations associated with the product or service that typically arise in people's minds. These include employees of the brand owner, those involved in the distribution, sale or supply of the product or service and ultimately the customers.

A few years ago Xerox realized the expectations associated with them were out of sync with the modern Xerox In creating a new brand, Xerox was hoping its visual identity would help the company image catch up with the philosophical changes the modern Xerox represents.

Xerox has not been a "copier company" for years, having grown beyond that and into networked printing solutions. However, a brand identity is more than a change in philosophy and it is more than a logo. Forging a brand identity starts with a scientific process of learning what is meaningful to your customers. Xerox spent more than 18 months preparing for the change by interviewing customers around the world about what associations they made with the Xerox name. They worked to retain the good things and get rid of the bad things. In the end, they were able to add attributes like modern, innovative, and flexible.

The point is that brands are about the entire package. As ForwardFast suggests, the brand links together the qualities of industry reputation (Likeability), visual impact (Logo), caliber of products (Quality Offering), connections to meaningful partners (Associations), brand personality (Attitude), and product interactions (Quality Experience). The way customers analyze all of these elements as a whole is what they perceive as your brand identity.

The ForwardFast tool diagrams, defines, and evaluates a brand. It is a framework through which you can look closely at key aspects of your brand. The goal is to learn what your brand really stands for and the attitude it projects, then to understand what positive brand associations can be created. By going through this process, you can make the shift from brand memorability to brand loyalty.

This part is designed as a mini-workshop and will give you a preview of the ForwardFast tool in action. Our approach is straightforward and simple. It is focused to reveal not only where your brand is, but also where it could be in the future.

The first step is to identify the most appropriate "action" to help you move your brand forward in the most expeditious and relevant manner.

Within this workshop, I have organized the exercises by these 6 key brand attribute points: likeability, logo, quality offering, associations, attitude, and quality experience.

PLAY

Chapter 6:

Likeability

Likeability is about approachability and personality. But how do you measure that? Consider the dating site, eHarmony. It is in the business of identifying and matching personalities. What if you could enter into the personality traits of your brand and compare them against actual or hypothetical customer attributes? Like eHarmony, you could match customers to your brand and find out who your market is and what they like. You could identify your "Big C" customer. That would be a powerful tool.

In the initial part of this chapter, I will begin to spell out brand traits that form the foundation of brand development. I start by defining why audiences are attracted to the brand. Then I gather a range of positive qualities to incorporate into the brand "story." Once you relate to the core brand traits – the defining aspects of the brand that remain largely unchanged – you can then discover vital brand attributes that can be developed over time based on learning and experience.

First, what makes a brand likeable? I believe customers look at brands like they look at people. They consider how they are treated by a brand, whether the brand is a good partner. In the same way a person might determine if someone is a good friend or not, they select which brands they like.

There are several ways to conceptualize likeability. One perspective is that it is the internal traits the brand strives to live up to. It also might be described as industry reputation and general awareness of the brand. Either way, it is measured by analyzing internal and external customer listening findings.

At the core, branding has a lot to do with this simple concept: Does the customer like the brand? But what sounds simple and straightforward can be a difficult thing to accomplish.

One medical ad agency has earned quite a reputation for creating characters or spokes-animals for drug clients. In the same way that Leo Burnett Advertising created characters for Kellogg's and Green Giant, this agency is known for, among other characters, a talking stomach, a dancing pancreas, and a kangaroo. They have readership studies for ads to show these are appealing, at least to attract attention. But likeability is more than just warm-and-fuzzy and cute. I have also seen an antibiotic like Cipro achieve likeability based on its performance in a wide range of infectious conditions. Therefore, it has earned its place as a tablet, IV, ophthalmic solution, and pediatric suspension. All of this without a cartoon character.

Another likeability example, this one from my own case files, is EMD/Merck Biosciences. This is a company that primarily sells research reagents – chemical "tools" that scientists use in drug discovery. They have catalogs filled with technical terms like pseudoproline dipeptides, hydrazino functionalized resins, and mitochondrial permeability-transition reagents. The issue at hand was how to attract people to look at the products they needed. EMD/Merck Biosciences wanted to convey that it was an interesting team to work with, not just a catalog filled with serial numbers. To achieve this, they used a series of high-quality nature photography – images of exotic plants, rare insects, and distant planets. These photographs carried the metaphor that the client needed, and they made the difference in getting people to look at the products.

Pharmaceutical branding is a delicate balance between creating likeability and communicating scientific viability. That's why it is so important that the consultancy that develops your branding understands the scientific concept of your product.

The case of Reolysin, a reovirus that attacks and destroys cancer cells, is a perfect example of a product that achieved this balance. In essence, administering this treatment involves infecting the patient with a virus. And when you are talking about infecting a person who is already sick with cancer, it is a tough pill to swallow. Oncolytics Biotech, the company that makes Reolysin, understood the difficult position they were in. They conducted extra-long clinical trials to prove conclusively that the product not only worked, but also that it was safe.

Pharmaceutical branding also has an unusual target audience. For the most part, the audience is scientifically savvy. But drugs also have a public persona. And with all of the recent "Big Pharma" public image issues of late, controlling the brand identity of products, especially new products that utilize new science, is vitally important. Some questions people consider about a brand include:

- Do the employees maintain a positive, optimistic attitude even when things are going very badly?

- Do I feel comfortable informing the company of my problems with the brand?

- Is the brand able to help me accomplish my goals?

- Is the company honest and trustworthy?

- Do I respect the company and what it does?

- Do I trust the company to make a good product?

- Is the brand able to help me accomplish my goals?

- Is the company communication honest and forthcoming?

- Is the customer service department responsive to my needs?

- Does the company listen to customers?

- Do I respect the company?

- Do I trust the company?

Keep these questions in mind when you consider how customers feel about your brand.

In addition to helping you assess the relative likability of your brand, compare your mission statement of purpose to other well-known brands like these:

- **Avon** – to be the company that best understands and satisfies the product, service, and self-fulfillment needs of women globally

- **eBay** – provide a global online marketplace where practically anyone can trade practically anything, enabling economic opportunity around the world

- **Google** – organize the world's information and make it universally accessible and useful

- **HSBC** – by connecting customers to opportunities, we enable businesses to thrive and economies to prosper, helping people fulfill their hopes and dreams and realize their ambitions

- **IKEA** – to create a better everyday life for the many

- **Mayo Clinic** – to inspire hope and contribute to health and well-being by providing the best care to every patient through integrated clinical practice, education, and research

- **Patagonia** – build the best product, cause no unnecessary harm, use business to inspire and implement solutions to the environmental crisis

- **Ritz Carlton** – our experience enlivens the senses, instills well-being, and fulfills even the unexpressed wishes and needs of our guests

- **Virgin Atlantic** – to grow a profitable airline, where people love to fly and where people love to work.

To tap into likeability, I recommend using brand stories. Humans have a natural affinity with stories. We like to tell stories. We like to hear stories. And most important to the task at hand, we like to explain things through stories. The first step in writing a brand story is coming up with a group of core brand traits that describe what your brand stands for. You are trying to build a personality here, so try to think of the same kind of words that you would use to describe a close friend. These are some of the typical core brand traits a story will highlight:

- Adaptable

- Communicative

- Optimistic

- Intuitive

- Respectful

- Passionate

- Curious

- Value-driven

- Trustworthy

- Vivacious

- Expressive

- Goal-oriented

- Kind

- Energetic

- Ambitious

- Leader

- Secure

- Altruistic

- Engaging

- Persistent

- Supportive

- Independent

- Involved

- Educated

Like any well-crafted story, there are four basic elements of brand storytelling: the message, the conflict, the characters, and the plot.

The message is important, especially in the type of storytelling health and tech brand teams are employing. You want to communicate some information about your company, and that is the message. Keep it simple, and keep your stories to one-message ideas.

The conflict is the element of the story that is a call to action. This is the thing that needs to be solved, the essential disharmony that needs to be put back into balance. Again, keep this simple and direct.

The characters are another essential part of your story. They can take any form you desire, but at the core, there should be a hero pursuing a goal. There might be other characters: supporters, adversaries, etc.

The plot is the progression of the story. The basic structure of the plot should start with the hero and his goal. The conflict is then introduced and pushes issues to the breaking point. At this point, the hero makes some kind of decisive choice that directly impacts the outcome of the story. Finally, the hero confronts the villain – the main obstacle to success – in the climax of the story. After this, the tension fades and the story draws to a close.

The point of this is to tell a story that illustrates the personality of your brand. Keep these elements in mind when writing your brand story:

- How does the story open?

- Who are the characters?

- What is the conflict and how is it introduced?

- What is the breaking point of the story?

- What is the climax of the story?

- How is the moral of the story presented?

As your brand story forms, begin to get a feel for your brand's personality, both as you conceive it and as it is seen from the outside.

Think about your brand, its personality, and how it is viewed by customers. Think about the traits you came up with and the story you developed. What are the key areas you can put effort into developing? What are the potentials of your brand's personality? What are inherent qualities that exist but are not being put in the forefront of your communication efforts?

Let's take a look at how likeability can form the basis of an entire ForwardFast brand model.

This story was written on a warm spring day in New Orleans by a select group of home care industry leaders convened in an historic

French Quarter hotel. Our goal was shaping the future of home care in the US. I was asked to lead a workshop that explored the rationale for a homecare brand identity that could improve awareness among all their stakeholders: patients, families, providers, and payers. I introduced the ForwardFast model for creating the home care industry brand.

In order to help the executives better describe the likeability of home care, I facilitated an exercise called PicSorting. Think of it as a way of putting your thousand words into a picture. In this workshop, there were 5-7 images arranged on the tables in front of participants. Each table selected one image based on their feelings in response to the prompt "Which image best represents how your clients feel about how home care could help their loved ones?" We used their stories to probe why those attributes would be likeable, and why they would be compelling to prospective families. Moreover, we compared and contrasted participants' stories to stimulate more feelings to move us toward a group consensus.

Through our discussions and interactive exercises, the industry leaders were able to build upon likeability to consider all six factors of ForwardFast branding:

- **Likeability** – the promise of both emotional and economic benefits.

- **Identity** – a bridge moving from chaos to order

- **Quality offerings** – what makes homecare different and how that difference is meaningful to customers

- **Attitude** – it's considered as the right thing to do and we are buttoned up

- **Brand associations** – the metrics, funding mechanisms, and certifications that would support home care

- **Quality experience** – one that is customizable, integrated, and coordinated. A combination of communications technology plus passion equals "comm-passion."

Through the thought-provoking collaborative session, we paved the way to establishing a consensus around the challenges and opportunities of the homecare industry. Participants left with clear action items that will help define a process to build momentum for a successful future.

In conclusion, likeability can be a powerful factor in branding. When you consider your brand, think of it as you would think of a person and define what makes it approachable and compelling. Use this set of core brand traits to develop a brand story. And when you have a sense of your brand's story, apply that to think about the core brand attributes that you can leverage and develop over time.

Chapter 7:

Logo/Identity

Now that you have a likeable brand with a great story, it is time to consider the face of that brand. In brand-speak, that is called the logo.

Logos are incredibly important to the identity of the brand. They must represent everything about the brand at a glance, and they have to do so gracefully, without forcing the connection. There must be a natural and logical connection between the logo and the brand.

Of course, a great logo starts with a great name.

I developed the launch campaign for Cozaar (losartan potassium) and Hyzaar (losartan potassium with hydrochlorothiazide). These products had great names with typography that helped illustrate the claim of a new class of angiotensin-II receptor blockade, so my creative team integrated it in the ad for the launch. The drugs achieved market leadership very rapidly and maintained it for a decade. Later when DuPont Pharma was sold to Bristol-Myers Squibb, DuPont retained its interest in Cozaar and Hyzaar trademarks which continue to be used worldwide.

After the name comes the brand symbol. I led the team that created the brand symbol for Advicor – a combination of time-release niacin and lovastatin in once-a-night dosage. It provides stronger cholesterol modulation by increasing HDL cholesterol and lowering LDL, triglycerides (TG), and lipoprotein-a. Our brand development groups created a story of "multidimensional lipid management" and a visual identity of a 4-D gyroscope, which is a device used for balancing forces. Based on our market research, it achieved the highest message recall and relevance of any brand tested at that time. The group coined it the lipidscope.

Building on the foundation of multidimensional lipid management my team created, Kos Pharma sought to expand medical applications for Advicor. One successful application was an effective treatment for cholesterol modulation in patients with metabolic syndrome.

I'm often asked, "What's a good story worth?" Well, here is one measure of value. In 2006, Abbott Laboratories acquired Kos Pharma for $3.7 billion in order to add Advicor and Niaspan to its arsenal. Abbott also gained the rights to another cholesterol-lowering medication Simcor, a new combination pill.

By definition, the logo is a type treatment and/or brand mark that represents the company. The logo also encompasses the brand name, which is as important as the brand mark because of the importance people place in words. In essence, the logo is a mental place-holder for the brand. It is a small element, but is incredibly important. It is the first thing people see and the last thing they remember. As I said, it is the face of the brand.

A good logo is both visually stimulating and tells a story about the company or brand. A perfect example is the television network CBS' logo: its iconic eye represents the company's eye for news and entertainment. Citigroup's logo is also representative of what they do – moving people from dreams to reality – and movement is integral to their logo.

One exciting project was the development of the logo family of Inoveon, a company devoted primarily to the fight against sight loss due to diabetic retinopathy and macular edema. In this case, the corporate logo had been already established, so my design partners built a brand family of products, services, reports, manuals, and documentation. As the company prepared an expansion strategy to new, large primary care practices, Inoveon wanted to place eye-screening systems to help monitor patients for diabetic retinopathy. My creative team helped produce a complete corporate identity system, using a series of their trademark services (iScan, iScore, iContact, iSight). The team also applied the logo system to a dimensional direct marketing effort to the top 1000 large group practices – linking to its updated website and its online testing report template. This was complemented by a 5-part lead generation and sales training system designed to help field representatives be more productive and effective in reaching the busy practice executives of large medical groups. Capitalizing on the established identity, our client successfully expanded the presence of the Inoveon brand.

Logos are not just static visual images. They embody the brand, and everything about them should serve that function. In other words, don't just think about the look of the logo. Consider the texture, the movement, the sound, the smell, and even the taste. This is the 5-D sensory experience I talked about in Chapter 2.

One of my most rewarding and meaningful projects of the last few years is a public service campaign for the Native American Children's Alliance. NACA is an inter-tribal membership organization whose mission is to promote excellence in child abuse prevention and intervention in Native American and Alaskan Native communities through training, mentoring, and information. Together with NACA, we helped to develop and execute a pilot initiative among key American

Indian healthcare clinics. The goals were to:

- Better understand the current circumstances around child abuse

- Develop culturally appropriate key messaging

- Develop appropriate and usable training and awareness kits for distribution

- Create key findings that could apply to a broader tactical awareness media campaign

My creative design partner, Katie Pendlay, developed three wonderful and touching concepts, each leveraging the NACA logo of a drum. Working through the executive director of NACA, Linda Logan, we evaluated these platforms at the Indian Health Services clinic in Chicago. They helped determine which tools were most needed. The result was a disk of customizable promotional assets: a poster, a tear pad easel, and a brochure. The campaign launched with tribes in rural New Mexico and in urban Detroit, then rolled-out to an Indian Nation conference held in Montana.

The goal for a logo is to express the entire brand experience. In a glance, your logo needs to project the emotion of the customer experience. "Play" companies use tried and true logo lockup techniques. "ForwardFast" companies need to do more.

This process applies another of my tools, A2U, to assess the awareness, attitude, and usage of your brand's logo. What do I want my audience to be aware of? What is the attitude I want my logo to present? And how do I want them to use this information? The first step is to examine the creative rationale of your current brand. Research the use of the brand name and logo both internally and externally, considering:

- Typography

- Color

- Symbol

- Descriptor

- Tagline

- Placement

- Uniformity of use

A2U can help you clarify marketing research objectives, organize your thoughts and objectives, ensure specific outcomes, make decisions based on key market information, identify trends or shifts in customers' attitudes, awareness or usage of the product, and identify feelings about the brand. If you are going to craft the best logo for your brand, these are all very important things to be clear about.

A discussion of logos can't be limited to print design. I think back to my days as a radio DJ when jingles were an audio logo for brands. Those are good memories working at radio stations in my hometown of Shreveport, Louisiana. But jingles have marketing power beyond nostalgia. In the golden age of ad jingles, the mere mention of some of the brands – Mentos, Kit Kat, Folgers or Oscar Mayer – was likely enough to get one of their ditties stuck in your head for the rest of the day. But jingles are a tactic not used much in mainstream advertising anymore, with some notable exceptions like Nationwide and McDonald's. This is in part because times — and media consumption habits — have changed. "Today's consumers are no longer couch potatoes who spend the majority of their lives in front of TV screens. They're mostly on mobile devices, mostly on the move, and always trying to get things done: uploading statuses to Facebook, searching for directions, reading articles, sharing photos [and] rating restaurants," Joe McCambley, senior vice president of content marketing at Pop said in ADWEEK. "It's an on-demand world where consumers choose to opt out of advertising either by skipping pre-roll video ads after three seconds, or blocking ads altogether via ad blockers. Where TV provided a captive audience and lent itself to jingles, mobile consumers refuse to be sold [to] and demand to be helped."

In addition to habits changing, consumer attention spans are more limited. "I'm not sure our visual, thumb-scrolling, auto-muted culture is set up to appreciate such brand communication," added Mark Mulhern, president of the East region at digital marketing agency iCrossing. "But that hasn't stopped the likes of Old Spice from introducing its own whistle in recent years – something they continue to embrace because it's working for them and their audience." Further, a catchy tune was a clever device when marketing channels were more limited, noted Mark Young, CEO of advertising agency Jekyll and Hyde Advertising. "You could run a significant amount of media on the few TV or radio networks that existed and within a reasonable time own a jingle that people could remember," he added. "Today we have hundreds of TV networks, thousands of radio options, millions of podcasts and even more websites to visit. Now compound this with social media and you have something akin to Digital ADD happening."

The average consumer receives 5000 to 20,000 brand messages a day and it's simply impossible for marketers to flood every available channel to the point a jingle becomes memorable. "This is why you are seeing old jingles resurrected because they came from a time when this was possible — the advertiser is drawing on warm, nostalgic memories," Young added.

But beyond simply tapping into fond memories, here are five reasons marketers shouldn't dismiss the humble jingle as irrelevant in the digital era:

1. Audio is an effective marketing tool. In addition to jingles, look no further than the use of pop songs in advertising like, say, Train's 'Hey, Soul Sister'. "That is because [they have] built-in familiarity and emotional connection," Young says. "It is much easier today to draw on a well-loved song and attach it to your product, transferring the feelings and emotions of the song to the brand." For his part, McCambley says he thinks we'll also see a resurgence of audio branding or sound trademarking in mobile, including tones or notes that consumers immediately associate with brands like AT&T, Skype, and Nokia.

2. Jingles can also drive consumer recall. "A jingle is a uniquely identifiable audio clip that works much in the same way

as a brand's tagline or even a brand's logo," according to Matt Lee, director of marketing at brand development and inbound marketing agency Adhere Creative. And the best jingles reinforce messages like brand promise, heritage, and consistency, says Scott Davis, chief growth officer at strategic consultancy Prophet.

3. Jingles, like pop music, are easy to remember. Jingles are arguably the only branding element with the power to get stuck in our heads. "Jingles still work for the same reason they worked in the past," says Michal Strahilevitz, associate professor of marketing at Victoria University. "Be it a jingle or a pop song, if you play a catchy tune with cute lyrics over and over again, people remember it."

4. Jingles cut through noise. Jingles can still be used to break through the clutter of our oversaturated, always-on, highly competitive world and simultaneously give consumers a feeling of familiarity and comfort. "Given the competitive state for a consumer's attention – anything that will give an edge to break through, grab attention and support brand recall is vital," comments Daniel Lobring, managing director of communication at integrated sports marketing agency rEvolution. "With consumers watching — or more likely just listening to — video ads, TV ads, Internet radio ads, etc., chances are that a memorable hook versus a straight copy read will grab their attention, good or bad. In some ways, the jingle becomes the hashtag or boilerplate. Think McDonald's 'I'm Lovin' It' or Kit Kat's 'Gimme a Break' —

in many ways you expect to hear it at the end of a spot. It creeps into your subconscious."

5. Jingles are manipulative. Shmuli Rosenberg, CEO of marketing and media firm fwd/NYC agrees music has a way of embedding messages in the consumer psyche. "When words are put to music their meaning is amplified, and they become much more potent and powerful," he said. "We teach young children through music and song. Nursery rhymes help children learn to form sentences, and we remember these for a lifetime. Using this tool has contemporary marketing power as it always has and always will." But it's also because jingles activate multiple brain lobes simultaneously, notes Brandy Miller of communications firm Creative Technology Services. "The motor center is activated in order to process the rhythm, the auditory center is activated in order to process the sound, the language center processes the lyrics and the limbic system processes the overall emotional core of the song. It's a powerful recipe," she said.

Further, consumer psychologist and retail consultant Bruce Sanders, author of "Sell Well: What Really Moves Your Shoppers," notes the durability and effectiveness of jingles lie in what media scientists call drumbeats. "Rhythmic elements build credibility in the brain. Rhythmically rhyming claims are more likely to be perceived as true than those that do not have this attribute," Sanders says. "Any Southern Baptist minister and most campaigning politicians could have told the scientists the value of rhyming jingles. The rhythm soothes our defenses and the repetition of sounds lends the sort of familiarity we associate with truth. Further, the rhythm energizes us, and energy, even if expended in inefficient ways, can give us the perception of success."

In conclusion, the logo is possibly one of the most important pieces of communication about your brand that customers will have access to. It carries the entire personality of the brand with it. It is an element that becomes so tied to a brand that the brand itself would be lost without it. What would Apple be without its eponymic apple? Or Nike without its swoosh? Or BMW without its signature round badge? These brands have a lot invested in their logos.

And so should yours.

Chapter 8:

Quality Offering

Quality Offering refers to a brand's promise of a particular quality to the consumers. It is a social contract between the company and the client. It represents both the product offerings — what you are actually selling — and quality claims — what you say you are selling. Your brand must provide a product that is useful to the consumer, and it must also make good on its quality claims. Remember likeability? Remember how that is built in part on trust? Well, if your product does not live up to its promise, you're sunk. That's why paying attention to quality offering is quite important.

I suggest using two exercises to evaluate the brand's services and programs, how they function, how they serve brand users and the medical or scientific community, and most importantly, how they contribute to the brand's vision. First, evaluate the value proposition of the brand. Second, identify key points of difference to competitors. Both of these processes are done using substantive, quantifiable data.

Even with strong medical and clinical data, sometimes the brand innovation processes can uncover surprising and useful performance characteristics of a product. This is the challenge faced with the arthritis drug, DayPro. When I teamed up with a branded science medical writer, we leveraged a heretofore underappreciated fact we discovered in the literature: DayPro could self-regulate its buildup in the body and avoid over-accumulation. We coined that self-regulation "compensatory clearance." This discovery allowed us to promote a campaign to take the drug once-a-day, every day to help prevent arthritis pain – not just as a treatment when it flared up. Our branded tagline memorably stated "Daylong Confidence, Proactive Intervention." Over the next 3 years, the business saw a reverse in market share decline and more than

20% increase in sales. That's the power of brand innovation.

What difference can actual efficacy make in the branding of a drug? Back in the cholesterol wars of Lipitor versus Zocor versus Pravachol, one analyst wrote in 1999. "There is a lot of growth left in Pravachol, but there is still a fair amount of growth left in Zocor. However, Lipitor has really slowed down all of the other product. It is clearly the fastest growing of the 3. Warner-Lambert's drug Lipitor is viewed as being the most potent at reducing cholesterol levels. Dose per dose it gives you the biggest benefit," written in Advertising Age November 8, 1999, quoting Jeff Chaffkin, a pharmaceutical analyst for Paine Webber. The Lipitor team continued the long-term brand strategy of making efficacy the primary measure – and ultimately dominated the market.

The implementation of Quality Offering applies another one of my tools: C.H.E.M., a communication device that teaches you to connect with your customers, to do so honestly, to give them an easy path, and to leave them motivated to experience your brand. It is a scientific process in the form of a checklist that focuses creativity for a specific function and allows everyone on the team to see the larger picture.

Let's look at each part of C.H.E.M. more closely.

- **Connect:** Who are you trying to connect with? How does it connect to the customer? Are you fitting into their life? Connecting is more than chit-chat. It's meaningful and relevant chemistry that you can build with your audience.

- **Honest:** Are you using the best facts and data? Are you making true claims? Establish an information exchange that allows you to introduce external points of view into a discussion and enables your audience to open up and share their situation or complaint with an issue.

- **Easy:** Is the communication easy to read? Easy to understand? Easy to navigate? Focusing on simplicity enables you to introduce potential solutions to your audience's situation as they've identified it, and enables them to easily and clearly understand the value of your solution. Motivate: Are you showing the customer how to take action? Directing them to where they want to go? Motivation encourages action by offering your audience a clear and easy first step toward their goal.

Brands add value to your company and products. I discussed that in Chapter 1. Value proposition is a term that refers to the performance and prices your brand promises to potential customers. It is, in a way, your pact with the customer, something you are assuring your constituents they will receive. What is the value your brand promises? What does your product guarantee your customers? Compare this to what you think your customers expect to get out of the brand. What do they think your product guarantees?

How do these considerations alter your business directive? Is your perception of your value proposition different from that of your customer? The impact of an inconsistency in these expectations can be very damaging to the perceived quality of your brand.

Ultimately, to show your brand's quality offering, you need to identify why your product is the one to buy.

Another example from my branding portfolio is Privigen, a ready-to-use 10% liquid IgG preparation, requiring no reconstitution. Because of its stabilizer proline, Privigen contains low levels of dimers, fragments, and aggregates. It does not contain sugar or preservatives and contains only trace amounts of sodium. The safety of Privigen resulted from a combination of advanced purification and pathogen inactivation/removal technologies. There had never been a confirmed reported case of pathogen transmission with Privigen. The R&D work showed that, unlike glycine-stabilized IVIg products that are approved for room temperature storage for 6 or 24 months, Privigen maintains efficacy and stability at room temperature for up to 36 months. The benefit of room temperature stability to the hospital pharmacist is that it eliminates the need for special refrigerated storage facilities, and importantly, allows immediate infusion without the need to warm the solution to room temperature prior to administration. The foundation of R&D branding became a key reason Privigen became the number one IVIg used in US hospitals.

Here's a little thought experiment for you to complete. Make a list of the key points of difference between your brand and your competitor's brand. In other words, what does your brand offer that your competitors lack? This could be a different feature, a different location, or a different type of employee. Consider elements that are quantifiable in nature, things you can count and measure.

Need some examples? Here are some ideas for differentiating elements:

- **Publications** – these add quantifiable credibility to your brand identity

- **Science** – like publications and education, scientific accomplishments lend credence to your claims

- **Education** – your involvement and commitment to education can make you stand out

- **Technology** – using innovative media for education, publications, and science

- **International** – accomplishments abroad can carry a lot of weight among some customers

- **Career** – employees make the brand, and you should highlight them if they are standouts

- **Membership** – key members of your organization who impact the value of your brand

- **Meetings** – where are they, what do they cover; try to think about what makes it special

In the weeks following the publication of my first edition of ForwardFast, I had a chance to pressure test the concept of quality offering in a marketing strategy program with our client, CSL Behring. The program was facilitated by Kevin Lane Keller of the Tuck School of Business at Dartmouth College. In our first session on strategic brand management and communicating the value of a brand, Keller noted that the power of brands is that they offer a promise to customers as a means to set their expectations. A strong brand, he said, improves marketing effectiveness and efficiency. In addition, a strong brand is one of the firm's most valuable assets. This concept of customer-based brand equity can create a real differential effect. In fact, customer brand knowledge is not necessarily just a set of brand or product facts, but rather a customer's response to the brand's marketing.

The marketing group looked at the determinants of customer-based brand equity and found that customers being aware of and familiar with the brand was just the beginning. In fact, brand equity extends to strong, favorable, and unique brand quality in the minds of the customer. With that foundation, the quality offering would create positive brand equity so the product would enjoy greater brand loyalty and be less vulnerable to competitive marketing actions. A product might command larger margins and even be more inelastic to price increases and more elastic to price decreases. It can increase communication effectiveness, yield licensing opportunities, and even support brand extensions. This idea of a customer-based brand equity based on the quality offering is really a bridge from added value to greater direction and focus to future marketing activities.

The Tuck School of Business proposed eight keys to achieving brand excellence:

1. Consumer-centric brand vision and passion.

2. Superior brand positioning vis-à-vis competition.

3. Clearly defined brand architecture.

4. Fully integrated marketing programs.

5. Cultivated brand relationships.

6. Premium-driven pricing strategies.

7. Relevant marketing innovation.

8. Well-managed brand growth strategies.

In achieving this quality offering in brand excellence, the consumer-centered brand vision and passion means a thorough and up-to-date consumer and employee understanding. The higher purpose that's anchored in consumer aspirations and the company's capabilities and goals transcends the physical product category descriptions and boundaries. The case study of Nike illustrated a large vision of bringing inspiration and innovation to every athlete in the world. The Nike brand values were to inspire, innovate, focus, connect, and care. The internal brand mantra of authentic athletic performance is translated into the external brand tagline, the well-known "Just do it".

In achieving brand excellence, a superior competitive positioning is paramount. These unique brand points of difference would be desirable to the customer, deliverable by the brand, and differentiated from the competition. It establishes brand points of parity, but also establishes and ensures brand duality to separate functional product performance and emotional brand imagery. The case study of Visa demonstrated this point. Of course, Visa is everywhere you want to be, but its goal is to attack American Express and marginalize Mastercard.

To neutralize and differentiate, it provides a point of differentiation — its acceptability and convenience — along with points of parity — status, prestige, and cachet. The tactics implied are a larger merchant network, gold and platinum cards, and worldwide acceptance.

To illustrate how quality offering is executed in fully integrated marketing programs, the group used the case study of Red Bull. Red Bull creatively combines sales generation and brand building in all of its marketing activities. It blends the consumer-directed pull with the channel-directed push to create a 360-degree mix-and-match marketing program that employs a range of traditional and non-traditional marketing activities, all coordinated to leverage its effects.

During our workshops with the clients, we were able to apply the classic brand positioning statement framework to the client's brand portfolio. The classic positioning statement is:

- To a target, group,

- Brand, is the frame of reference, perceptual,

- competing mainly with

- that, relevant differentiating benefit,

- because, reason to believe.

This exercise in brand positioning gave our brand teams a better appreciation of how we want to target customers to think about brands with respect to competitors. It also provided strong brand positioning to guide organizational activities and budgeting to clarify the brand's essence to help the customer achieve solutions to their problems.

In conclusion, we as a team appreciated how to create powerful brands and that it required an organization-wide commitment to collectively develop and implement state-of-the-art branding practices. We saw what it took to excel at all brand marketing competencies, and we were more assured that our marketing decisions could work together to maximize brand value. This builds on the strategic brand management concept of quality offering.

In conclusion, consider this: your product's quality is only as good as your customers think it is. Your goal, in forging a brand identity, is to make sure that the true value of your brand is seen by the customer. The goal is to hit the target dead on – too little value and your customers don't see what they are getting; too much and they may end up disappointed. You strive to create a quality offering – make sure your customers understand that quality.

FORWARDFAST

Chapter 9:

Associations

Associations are perhaps one of the most difficult branding concepts to grasp, but they are an important aspect of the ForwardFast model. Brand associations are memorable links between your brand and other things, much like the "Blue Light Special" is associated with K-Mart, or iTunes with Apple. Associations are important because they improve the value of your brand – enhancing loyalty and increasing brand recall.

As an illustration in the pharma world, let's look at the Novartis Foundation for Sustainable Development. The advances of the Pharma industry mean very little if the drugs don't get to the sick people. And in third-world countries, crushing poverty and rampant malfeasance often prevent proper distribution of drugs to the people who need them. Recognizing a need, Novartis created a foundation that focuses on providing "pioneering health projects in developing countries aimed at achieving specific goals in the fight against poverty and disease as well as at inspiring and improving development policy and practice." One of the ways Novartis achieves their goals is through educational events. They recognize that the efforts must be taken to the people and into the remote villages. It is not just about drug costs and drug supplies. Access is an important key, as is education. These events are a powerful tool in energizing a group to action. By creating a compelling presentation — using language that is meaningful to your audience — you can achieve maximum message effect. The impact of groups can be felt through a powerful personal connection, and this method is often more meaningful than print materials or visual representations. Involvement is a key aspect to the power of the program as a brand association.

This chapter covers three main topics. First, I will expand on the definition of associations. Understanding what associations are and how they work is an important step to using them to your benefit. Second, I will talk about discovering connections to your brand and how to capitalize on those connections. This includes identifying possible subspecialties you can highlight with associations. Finally, I will explore areas where you can add associations, which means connecting your brand with specific services or external programs. By the end, you should have a good idea of the value of associations and a clear picture of ongoing and future association opportunities.

Three companies I have had the pleasure to work with have used associations particularly well: Eli Lilly, Westwood (a dermatological division of Bristol-Myers Squibb), and Alcon (a producer of ophthalmological and eye care products). Each of these companies has a history of product innovation in their respective therapeutic areas, as well as years of relationship-building with customers.

They each recognized that they could extend their brand beyond just the company and its products. These are just a couple of examples of associations that can be made:

- Eli Lilly created special disease recognition and awareness among ethnic groups that had a higher propensity for diabetes.

- Westwood created a robust scholarship program for residents. Applicants wrote a dermatological science paper to be judged by a panel and the winners presented their papers at a major meeting. They were also awarded key office tools and textbooks.

- Alcon developed a blindness-prevention campaign in cooperation with ORBIS and the World Health Organization's Vision 2020 program.

- Each of these is an example of not only good corporate citizenship, but also smart brand associations.

Four key characteristics define associations. One, they are links between a brand and something else – links that enhance the memorability of that brand. Two, associations may or may not be linked to something that actually exists – a link could be to a symbol like the golden arches or to an actual organization like the Ronald McDonald House. Three, associations can be measured by strength level, so you can have strong or weak associations. And four, associations are most effective when they are categorized into thematic groups. I'll take these one by one.

Associations are links. They are things that you encourage customers to associate with your brand. There is an endless list of possibilities here, but in general, it can be broken down into 9 categories:

1. **Characters** – these can be mascots, spokes animals, or even real people. Examples include the Colonel of Kentucky Fried Chicken, Billy Mays of OrangeGlo/OxiClean, the Marlboro Man, or Tony the Tiger of Kellogg's.

2. **Feelings** – any feeling can be linked to your product, such as happiness, fun, excitement. One recent campaign for Coke appealed to you to "Open Happiness."

3. **Characteristics** – such as the large foil-wrapped burrito for Chipotle.

4. **Service** – things that are special categories of what you do, like Amazon's recommendations or the Ronald McDonald House.

5. **Symbol** – this is a special link to an image, not necessarily your logo. Examples are the golden arches, Budweiser crown, etc.

6. **Lifestyle** – you can link your brand to a particular way of life. Starbucks, for example, creates this kind of association, as does Applebee's.

7. **Object** – this is a physical representation of the concept you wish to communicate, like the pink breast cancer ribbon or the yellow LiveStrong bracelet.

8. **Activity** – activity associated with the product – North Face is associated with outdoor activities. Bank of America wants to be strongly associated with the Chicago Marathon. Novartis is associated with educational events through their Foundation for Sustainable Development.

9. **Product** – product associations may also take the form of line extensions.

As you can see, some of these examples represent something real and others do not. This is the second quality of associations – they do not necessarily represent reality. Often associations with something real create stronger associations, but this is not always the case. Strong ties can be made to abstract concepts.

This leads to the third characteristic of associations – varying strength levels. Obviously, some associations are stronger than others, and which associations are strongest should be carefully controlled.

What makes strong links are the number of association experiences and the network of other supporting connections. The number of associations can mean a sense of longevity – such as the continuing presence of Orville Redenbacher (even after his death in 1995 with a digital recreation). But it can also mean a consistency of association – Starbucks strives to create an association with a certain type of attentive service every time a customer walks into the store.

A network of other connections can help support and strengthen any association. Apple's association with generating ideas is strengthened by associations with innovative products such as the iPod and the iPhone. Which leads us directly to the fourth characteristic of associations.

The most effective associations are clustered. This is illustrated by the example of line extensions, which are a product association with a new product. Generally, line extensions should be supported by an existing network of associations.

It feels nostalgic now to look back at the list BRANDWEEK published of the best and worst line extensions of 2007, illustrating this effect nicely. At the top were the PetSmart PetsHotel, Huggies Little Swimmers sunscreen, Disney's Fairy Tale wedding gowns, and American Idol camp. Each plays off of the original brand's existing qualities – pets, swimming, fairy tales, and singing. In contrast, in my opinion, the least desirable are examples of an extension trying to fly solo: Precious Moments coffins, Humane Society Dog Lovers Wine Club, and Girls Gone Wild apparel.

Now that you have a better idea of what associations are, I can share some applications. I'm sure you're already thinking of places where you are using associations and places where you could take advantage of this strategy.

The process for accessing association opportunities begins with a consideration of your specialty – your company's primary function. From there, you can move into all the things your company is involved in that are subspecialties of that primary function. Questions you should be asking in this exercise are:

- What subspecialties are you currently taking advantage of?

- What subspecialties make sense for you to expand into?

- Who can you partner with to make expansion more effective?

Once these questions are answered with examples specific to your current product offerings, look into programs and services that can be created. Though these fit into the scheme of association types, programs and services have a slightly different flavor. Instead of subspecialties of your brand's primary function, these are extra things you are involved with. For example, McDonald's is associated not only with Ronald McDonald, who is a subspecialty, but also with the Ronald McDonald House, a charitable organization, and the Children's Food and Beverage Advertising Initiative, a voluntary program regarding the advertising of healthy food choices at fast food restaurants. Notice, however, that these programs are still supported in the network of McDonald's associations with good things for children.

The current trend for clinical trial identity is to use it to create a brand association. The primary objectives of clinical trial identity are to define, communicate, differentiate, drive credibility, generate traction, and plant the seeds for launch brand growth. Clinical trial identity is but one of several phases of pre-launch initiatives of the drug development phase that might include scientific story, scientific glossary, INN name, clinical trial identity system, product positioning, brand positioning, brand name, and visual identity.

For example, in a recent bleeding-reversal-product trial, where four factors were balanced by a single agent, the trial is 4Balance. The 4Balance trial purpose is to evaluate the efficacy, safety, and tolerance of a PCC compared with plasma in patients who require immediate correction of INR.

In another case, AstraZeneca created an entire suite of trials based on a space theme – aptly named the Galaxy Program. This is a comprehensive, long-term, evolving, and global research initiative. Each trial in the program is named based on a space-related term and the entire program falls under a single branding design umbrella, complete with a logo template that allows for an individual logo for each trial.

A major program of cancer clinical trials my team helped brand is SURPASS. The name SURPASS describes how the pharma sponsor is going beyond available

Treatments in its pursuit of controlling cancer recurrence and improving survival. It offers patients and investigators renewed hope. At its initiation, the SURPASS Program consisted of two groups of clinical trials: VOYAGE and EMBARC, each name representing a group of investigative journeys for the treatment of bladder cancer using distinct molecules.

To leverage the concept of brand association, types of clinical trial names fall into several categories: Acronyms, real words, coined words, alpha-numerics, and more.

You can develop existing associations of this kind using publications, organizations, partners and charities that you are already affiliated with. Focus on these elements that service your primary customer base or that deal with your primary area of focus.

As I'm sure you can see, associations are powerful connections that have strong implications for enhancing your brand's value. I hope I have given you a good sense of what associations are and how you can use them to help move your brand ForwardFast.

Chapter 10:

Attitude

Do a Dew. Roll in a Beamer. Cruise on a Harley. Or Just Do It. Each of these brands has a unique personality and projects an attitude to their customer base. Mountain Dew is the extreme drink for extreme drinkers. BMW is the pinnacle of quality for the discriminating driver. And Harley Davidson is an American icon of road-tested thunder. Nike is the shoe of choice for professionals and not-so-professionals. Attitude is the "personality" of the brand and could be represented by a coined word or phrase. The best way to create a unique personality is to develop visual and verbal campaign hallmarks.

Attitude considers both the presentation of the brand to the consumer and the reception of that brand message. So you have to be aware of not only what you are projecting, but what your customers are reading – which are not always the same thing.

Why is attitude important? Because in order to send an effective message you must know what the attitude is on both sides of the equation. You also need to understand brand attitude in order to accurately measure progress toward the goals you set for marketing campaigns. In order to determine brand attitudes, search for and evaluate personality characteristics used to describe the brand, both by insiders and outsiders. In other words, find out what words or phrases people use to describe your brand.

The ultimate goal is to creatively express the brand attitude, but to do that you must honestly determine the existing prevalent attitude.

For example, I had the opportunity to work with a major medical laboratory services company. They achieved such a dominant position in the field of large lab analyses for hospitals and commercial testing centers that when they faced significant manufacturing quality and regulatory challenges, it sent ripples through the marketplace. This caused an incredible backlash from customers who had grown to count on the company for consistent supplies and products. The labs didn't know where else to turn, and this crisis for the company became a crisis for the customers.

In working with this client, my team helped develop a shift in brand attitude from dominance to empathy, common cause, and more mutual and collaborative problem-solving. While losses in both accounts and revenues were significant, this refined brand attitude is credited with helping achieve the needed rebound when order was eventually restored.

So you see, in order for our client to recover, they had to come to grips with the current prevailing attitude – one of dominance. They also had to come to realize that dominance of the marketplace, in this situation, ended up being a negative characteristic. They carried the entire burden of the marketplace on their shoulders.

This knowledge of current attitudes allowed us to have a clear point of origin, which not only allowed us to strategize forward movement but also gave us a benchmark by which to track our progress. And this let us apply the Strategic GPS® tool to plan out the brand attitude adjustment.

Referencing Tom Rath's StrengthsFinder 2.0, here is a list of personality characteristics you can apply to your brand. These are by no means the only characteristics you can use, but they do make a pretty good start:

Personality Characteristics You Can Apply to Your Brand

- Achiever

- Activator

- Adaptability

- Analytical

- Arranger

- Belief

- Command

- Communication

- Competition

- Connectedness

- Consistency

- Context

- Deliberative

- Developer

- Discipline

- Empathy

- Focus

- Futuristic

- Harmony

- Ideation

- Includer

- Individualization

- Input

- Intellection

- Learner

- Maximizer

- Positivity

- Relator

- Responsibility

- Restorative

- Self-Assurance

- Significance

- Strategic

A case study that illustrates telling a brand story from multiple vantage points is from my efforts for the national Arthritis Foundation. The Arthritis Foundation is the largest private, not for-profit contributor to arthritis research in the world, funding more than $470 million in research grants since 1948. It is the leading health organization addressing the needs of some 50 million Americans living with arthritis, the number-one cause of disability in the U.S. The mission of the Arthritis Foundation has been to improve lives through leadership in the prevention, control, and cure of arthritis and related diseases.

My agency's N-of-8 group process would guide messaging in PSAs, a new website, fundraising, direct marketing, and public relations. Groups of eight were conducted in four cities across the country. I wrote stories from the view of arthritis patients, families, physicians, disease symptoms, research, and the Foundation.

In the groups, patients experienced a dramatic shift from who feeling helpless or victimized, to those feeling empowered and in greater control of their lives. This led to the new tagline, "Arthritis Foundation: Take Control, We Can Help." What's more, it provided the impetus and direction for the Foundation to focus on its core strengths -- providing public health education; pursuing public policy and legislation to improve healthcare; and conducting evidence-based programs to improve the quality of life for those living with arthritis. It also revealed that constituents wanted specifics on the activities and results on Foundation programs.

This led to documentation of the nearly $20 million in grants to nearly 300 researchers, and the major treatment advances for most arthritis diseases resulting from the more than 50 years of research. Community-based programs and services gained renewed focus, including aquatics, exercise, and the clinically proven Arthritis

Foundation Self-Help Program. It also re-energized the grassroots advocacy at both the national and local level to advance critical legislative policy issues.

The next time you think about your brand, consider the attitude it projects. Listen to your customers, your shareholders, and your employees. All of these individuals have a different take on attitude, and they all have an impact on it. Are you positioned attitudinally to your best advantage?

Chapter 11:

Quality Experience

Any conversation about customer service always generates personal stories about a memorable experience you've had – at a restaurant, hotel, store, or airline. While bad experiences might stick in our minds, we just as often recall some wonderful moment when we were cared for and made to feel special.

If you take the time to study these experiences, you can learn from them – and even more important, learn how to replicate positive customer service in your business.

In the truest sense, a quality brand experience is created when a customer tells you what they want, and you respond to them in ways that integrate your brand into their life.

Let me share with you an excellent reference on this subject. A practical book entitled, DNA of Customer Experience: How Emotions Drive Value, by Colin Shaw. In his book, Shaw summarizes the underlying reasons to elevate your level of service, plus why it makes financial sense:

Why Improve the Customer Experience

1. Produce more loyal customers

2. Attract new customers at a lower cost

3. Reduce costly complaints as much as possible

4. Increase the value of your best customers

Why It Makes Financial Sense

- It is always cheaper to service current customers than prospect for new ones

- Word of mouth and referrals are cheaper than mass advertising

- Cutting waste and inefficiency adds profit right to the bottom line

- Loyal customers will spend more per order, place more orders, and spread the word

I have spent nearly two decades studying, creating, evaluating, and training on customer brand experiences. So, I appreciate the rigor of research conducted by the London Business School, which outlines four clusters of emotions that can impair value – or, if addressed, can actually add value, first let's look at the customer's feelings that can be destructive. These emotions are evoked in customers typically because their experience is "inside out". This means the business focuses more on what is good for it and less on the experience of the customer. The customers will describe feeling stressed, neglected, frustrated, disappointed, hurried, or irritated. As you improve service, you can start with simply engaging customers' attention. The research shows that you can encourage customers to explore your offerings – and boost their short-term spending – by doing things that make them feel stimulated, creative, energetic, and indulgent.

Moving up to the next level, customers will recommend your business if they feel valued, cared for, and trusted. Consider your own personal experience: something nice that someone might have done for you at home, at your child's school, or at a place you volunteer. What did the person do and why did you feel valued? It's probably because you know they spent time thinking about you, listening to you, understanding you, and personalizing a note or gift for you. Now expand this to the experience in your business, and think about what you could do for your best customers.

At the top of the pyramid are happy customers who become advocates. These are customers who feel happy, pleased, and even thrilled with their experience. They go beyond being the most loyal to proactively telling people about your business without prompting.

In chapter eight, I referenced a marketing management strategy program with our client, CSL Behring, in 2008. Our facilitator, Kevin Lane Keller of the Tuck School of Business at Dartmouth College shared several examples of how cultivating brand relationships through experiences is key to achieving marketing excellence. Quality experiences develop a customer pipeline by attracting new consumers and enhancing the loyalty of existing ones. It helps us understand the customer's lifetime value and helps us manage customer relationships long-term. Moreover, it helps establish rational and emotional components in marketing to create brand resonance.

There were several terrific examples of quality experiences and lessons to be learned for better improving experiences in the airline industry, including Singapore Airlines. This airline is building a strong foundation of service, quality, and performance by pampering customers in all classes to create positive experiences and feelings. This can be seen in its cabin ambience, dining, amenities, in-flight entertainment, ground services, and its loyalty programs. Compare that to your own experiences with flying other airlines.

In the healthcare industry, brand experience applications included Zyprexa from Eli Lilly, Blue Cross Blue Shield health insurance providers, and the Mayo Clinic in the hospital industry.

In applying these learnings to quality experience, you can see how a well-crafted brand positioning statement would not only target your customer and develop its competitive frame of claims, but also help guide the brand's experience activities by clarifying the essence of the customer's relationship with the brand at all touch points.

Are you ready? That is the question that Alli, the only FDA-approved diet pill, asks prominently on its website, MyAlli.com. "Have you got what it takes to follow the Alli™ program? Before you begin, be sure Alli is right for you. You don't just try Alli to see what happens. You have to commit to a plan that's realistic; one based on gradual weight loss." Honesty. What a concept. But this is a perfect example of branding – a quality offering combined with a quality experience. GlaxoSmithKline knows that there is no wonder pill that magically makes you skinny. And they know that consumers know that (even if they don't want to admit it). So they have designed the Alli brand with honesty as the cornerstone. You have to work to get thin. The OTC drug can help, "but it's more than just a pill. It's an innovative weight-loss program. The pill works by preventing your body from absorbing some of the fat you eat. And the program includes an individually tailored, online action plan to help you lose weight safely and gradually." By painting an honest picture, they are not creating false hopes. And by including the customer in the overall experience, they are tying that customer to the brand in a powerful way.

Changing habits and beating addictions is one of the most difficult things we do. Whether it is losing weight or quitting smoking, a drug alone is not enough – there has to be a support system. The branding for the Commit Lozenge offers not only a relief to cravings but includes on their website "My Quit Place" which provides a dosing calculator, a trigger detector, and a cravings pacifier, all of which are designed to help smokers break their habit. "Quitting is a process, not an event," the website tells us. Great advice like this appears all throughout the site. But my favorite is the Savings Calculator. This features lets you input the cost per pack of cigarettes and how many cigarettes you smoke each day. It then spells out how much money that costs you each day, week, month, and year. For a society that is very financially driven, this is a great addition to the raft of reasons to quit.

This is the kind of branding that could move more pharma products ForwardFast.

Let's take a closer look at some retail examples of brand experiences. Well-known companies including Starbucks, Crocs, and GAP are known specifically for their memorable experiential marketing tactics.

These three well-known brands have done a great job of creating memorable brand experiences for their customers. Starbucks, Crocs, and GAP are all very different in what they provide to their customers;

however, they have one underlying similarity – the experience the customer encounters when interacting with their products.

STARBUCKS – the neighborhood gathering place

For Starbucks, the number one marketing strategy is opening stores. It considers the major media choice to be the baristas and the idea of creating a neighborhood gathering place.

When creating experiential-marketing programs, Starbucks Vice President of Marketing Brad Stevens suggests you have to be guided by four key elements:

- Authenticity – the ability to see it, feel it, and taste it

- Human Connection – interacting at an emotional level

- Participation - creating a memorable experience that people will equate with your brand

Core focus

As it relates to the baristas at Starbucks in creating the ideal customer experience, part of the core focus is the training manual. Starbucks has created a training program to include "Five Ways of Being":

1. Be welcoming

2. Be genuine

3. Be knowledgeable

4. Be involved

5. Be considerate

There are many marketing tactics that have worked for Starbucks, as well as lessons learned from events and programs that did not work as planned. One example of a failed promotion during the holiday season is the use of magnetic coffee cups on cars. When a good samaritans would tell the owner of the car that a cup had been left on the hood, they would then be given a gift certificate to Starbucks for pointing it out.

Another idea was a crossword puzzle promotion in the various stores. The marketing team thought that since most people read the newspaper while in the store that a promotion tied around solving five NY-Times-level puzzles would appeal to the masses. This promotion did not take off and ended up with responses only in the hundreds. Starbucks realizes that, in order to stand out at an event, you cannot just be a sponsor. The sponsorship must be activated, as it did during Aspen Food & Wine Events. Starbucks conducted a tasting for coffees that had been created by chefs participating at the event. These were exclusive blends you could not get anywhere else. The response was fantastic and, therefore, leveraged their visibility at the event.

CROCS – strapping on to sponsorships

When the Crocs brand was new to the consumer, it needed to be experienced before it would be purchased. However, these shoes weren't attractive, so customer interaction could tell the bigger story. Crocs used a method of 360 degrees of activation with their sponsorships. This included their products, merchandise, and signage. Crocs realized its purchase is an experiential purchase. Crocs has made great strides in understanding its audience and focuses its marketing dollars on the highest impact, most cost-effective inventory. Crocs provides a great example of making a small budget play big for its size.

The Crocs brand has maximized its onsite experiential marketing opportunities at the various sporting events and shows in which they participate. They minimize traditional signage and integrate themselves into the event itself by activating the sponsorship in a fun way. They've given back to the consumer by creating pages such as crocs.com/running and by giving customers the opportunity to put their favorite sports team on the back strap of their shoes.

Overall, Crocs looked at their competitive environment and did something different.

They've expanded their products to cover every target demographic. They have caddies wearing their shoes during the PGA and writing a blog about their experience afterwards. It's a hot brand and getting hotter.

GAP – partnering for a cause

GAP has been a well-known retail clothing outlet for many years. They've been known to support various causes, but nothing that has truly set them apart from their competitors. In October 2006 with the help of Bono and Oprah, GAP launched their involvement with (PRODUCT) RED™ on Michigan Avenue in Chicago.

The launch event featured an overnight transformation of the GAP store on Michigan Avenue. They colored all of the windows red and brought in GAP employees from stores across the country for this launch.

Fifty-percent of the proceeds from GAP RED goes toward the Global Fund, started by Bono and Bobby Shriver, which helps women and children in Africa affected by HIV/AIDS. GAP has not only become a global partner of (PRODUCT) RED™, but they also contribute by having some of their clothing made in Africa.

In this same spirit, I can also share with you three of our own Brand Experience case studies.

Redefining the Donor Experience

With blood donations not increasing in years and blood centers looking for new creative methods to attract blood donors, my agency team planned a dinner symposium for blood bank executives around the idea of "Redefining the Customer Experience." The symposium consisted of speakers from name-brand customer service organizations including The Ritz Carlton, Disney Institute, and the author of The Starbucks Experience.

The forum included opportunities for executives to interact with the expert speakers as well as a book signing after the event. Executives left with ideas and education for enhancing the blood-donation experience.

Making sleep therapy a medical experience

Sleep diagnostics is practically a cottage industry. But our client, Total Sleep, wanted to present a different experience to their clients. They built their business on providing sleep lab services and medical equipment to diagnose and treat sleep apnea. They wanted to create a clinical medical experience for their clients, and by working with sleep experts they created an algorithm and clinical design that elevated the sleep diagnostic experience to a new level.

Packaging can also contribute to an improved customer experience. One of my brand design teams created a packaging system for Urocor Diagnostics that provided all the components necessary for prostate testing and biopsy collection. Each formalin-filled collection vial has a specific bar code for use with the kit. The vial insert spaces were labeled for biopsy locations in the recommended sextant technique. These design elements greatly increased the accuracy of the testing.

To take the pulse of the international experiential marketing community in regard to the definition of the methodology itself, the

Experiential Marketing Forum (EMF) conducted a survey of marketing and advertising professionals.

The results of this survey are not altogether shocking. The EMF found that the accepted definition and benefits of experiential marketing varies among professionals. It has certainly become a hot topic among marketing professionals, but potential clients are not sure what they are getting with this kind of treatment. Experiential marketing has become one of those phrases that really has no agreed upon meaning due to misuse.

Overall, experiential marketing represents the opportunity to address, and in some cases reconnect with, customers and potential customers in relevant and meaningful ways. Equally important, in a time of consumer-generated media and skepticism concerning conventional media, the experiential approach is treasured.

There are some areas of total agreement within the community of professionals who use this technique, but there remain points of difference. This is seen as normal by the EMF – a natural result of the evolution of this powerful tool.

Approaches and activities described as experiential marketing illustrate the wide variety of ways in which experiential marketing is being used. Approximately one-third of the respondents believed they consider experiential marketing to be the lifeblood and the core of their organizations. They describe it as the basic philosophy around which the services and products of their organization are built. Roughly half describe their organization's use of experiential marketing as a tool, referencing events and other activities that build relationships, engage prospects, stimulate trial, and create buzz. The remainder considers experiential marketing to be a frontier – an approach they might or might not explore, depending on their own courage and the appetite of their clients.

Only 13% of the respondents assumed that increased sales are the most significant result experiential marketing can deliver. The majority think engagement is the strong suit of experiential marketing. In their own words, professionals described the powerful impact of engagement as building relationships, creating a positive, real experience, building loyalty, increasing relevance, capturing attention, eliciting emotion, stimulating word-of-mouth, changing opinions, building trust, and increasing product desire. The concept of engagement has many dimensions, and professionals are articulate in specifying the particular dimension of engagement they look for in their campaigns and activities.

In addition, other interesting differences emerged. People whose professional responsibilities include evaluating experiential marketing are less focused on engagement, as a result, and more likely to expect it to deliver actions, such as word of mouth. As evaluators, they rely on results that can be measured.

People with no direct involvement in experiential marketing are less likely to mention the real experience and more likely to say they expect it will increase prospects' desire for more product. This leads one to believe that as more marketing professionals experience this type of campaign they will better understand the philosophy behind it.

Respondents reported that a well-executed experiential marketing concept can make respondents more receptive to other marketing, foster believability, and trust, motivate consumers with the urge to respond, stimulate voluntary brand engagement, use the conversation of interaction to convert prospects to customers, and transfer ownership of the brand to the consumer.

Professionals who plan, approve and implement experiential marketing place more emphasis on its potential to build relationships, produce interaction, verify the target audience, increase awareness, and increase sales. These folks, at the front lines of creating experiential marketing, place less emphasis on the potential of experiential marketing to generate trial, elicit emotion, create memories, or build loyalty. On the other hand, professionals whose responsibility is to evaluate experiential marketing place more emphasis on relevance, loyalty, trial and memory and less emphasis on relationship, interaction, WOM, and information.

Professionals are consistent in their association of Experiential Marketing with "sensory experience," "interaction," and "relationship." In selecting five words that best describe experiential marketing from a list of 15, over three-quarters of the respondents selected one or more of these words. "Memories" were associated with experiential marketing by nearly half the respondents.

The relative strength of each of the 15 words associated with experiential marketing was determined by weighting top-ranked words proportionately to lower or unranked words. Within the total number of votes available to all respondents, the weighted rankings were indexed to 100. The community of international marketers who responded to the EMF survey voiced strong agreement in their selection of "Sensory experience," "Interaction," and "Relationship" as words to describe experiential marketing. "Consumption" and "Response" (the behavioral dimensions) received a small percentage of the ranking votes.

The middle-ranking words, such as "Memories," "Information," "Presence," "Immediate," "Response," "Context," "Trust," "Reward," "Community," and "Long-term," received votes from some, but not most, of the respondents.

Still, these words remain as very important aspects of experiential marketing. The concepts expressed by these words are recognized lynchpins around which many campaigns are created.

There is strong agreement that the big play of experiential marketing is engagement. However, there are differences of opinion in exactly what dimension of engagement is accomplished. People who implement experiential marketing have different expectations for its results than people who evaluate it.

Professionals who use experiential marketing are enthusiastic about its potential, although not without the caution that best practices in strategy and implementation must be followed.

Marketing professionals, as well as clients who are novices to experiential marketing, may have to mount a learning curve, which includes participation in experiential marketing, in order to understand and appreciate the significant engagement results that it can deliver.

Results of the joint research study show that experiential marketing is a rich and complex communication technique – and not a game for amateurs. Quality experiences are not only a good idea; they are a necessity in the current marketing environment. Flawlessly executed experiential marketing campaigns that reflect the creative strategy and the positioning and tone of voice of the brand require a well-rounded approach, according to survey respondents.

Experiential marketing is evolving and maturing. Some experiential marketing campaigns are more successful than others. That's why it is important that best practices are clarified. Industry generated benchmarks for success are vital.

Top objectives of experiential marketing campaigns:

- Build relationships

- Produce interaction

- Verify target audiences

- Increase awareness

- Increase sales

- Increase relevance

- Increase loyalty

- Increase trial

- Create memories

In one of my client training workshops, I benchmarked several successful brands that are design customer experience we can aspire to. Lego gives children the opportunity to play with their toys in shops and, even more so, letting parents experience their children having fun with Lego toys. Zara creates a sense of anticipation in their clothing shops, driving customers to repeat visits 17 times per year, compared to the 3-4 visits per year for regular stores. Build-a-Bear Workshop builds a brand experience with fun and unforgettable memories in a dramatic, highly interactive theme-park-esque environment with bright colors, larger-than-life fixtures, and customized music; all to encourage people to stay and interact with the products and the associates. My M&M's website customizes the popular chocolate candies which is a great way to add a personal touch to wedding and event favors, add some color to a birthday party, or give as a creative gift.

All of this reflects that there's a new rule of brand management. Through a brand, customers expect future utility on the part of the entire company. Managing the brand that has momentum and direction is now everyone's responsibility. Every link in the value chain needs to be devoted to the brand and the customer to align strategic decisions with product and service innovation, brand management, customer experience and marketing. To achieve this, the brand and its core team must be used as a basis for guiding the business forward rather than simply a brand-building communications function detached from business strategy.

These views are covered in detail in "Brand Bubble, the Looming Crisis in Brand Value and How to Avoid It," by John Gerzema and Ed Lebar. They outline the new world of brand management as driving the brand back through the organization instead of simply sending a brand into the marketplace. A company with an energized value chain constantly thinks, plans and acts from the viewpoint of the brand. Together these moves create a culture that is consistently championing creativity and embracing change.

Gerzema and Lebar also advocate active listening and constant refreshing of the brand name. Today, brands must be in a state of constant renewal. They must subject themselves to never-ending feedback. They must be ready to reshape themselves over and over again in whatever form that takes. Energized brands are leading, adapting, surprising, innovating, involving, and responding. Behaving differently at different times with different customers and collaborators is essential. With expanding customer power and limitless choice, brands cannot possibly stay the same for long.

In today's world, market position has never been more temporary. Success is often a momentary high followed by a tumbling fall. We must listen carefully to the market and learn from its mistakes in a forward-looking way. We must continuously modify, personalize, share and improve upon ourselves. Our brands must be an agent of constant surprise. The fact is everything is moving faster today, creating unparalleled pressure on brands to be quicker, smarter, leaner, more responsive and able to innovate more quickly.

A critical factor slowing momentum is often a need to protect and vet a sacred strategy. Strategic accuracy often trumps the need for the brands to respond to make customers change their needs. This inability to change lies at the heart of consumer discontent with so many stagnant and predictable brands.

There's another guideline of brand administration suggested by Gerzema and Lebar. Through a brand, clients expect future utility with respect to the whole organization. Dealing with the brand that has energy is everybody's obligation. Each connection of importance should be given to the brand and the client to adjust vital choices, to advance, to administer. To accomplish this, the brand and its central group must be utilized as a premise for directing the business forward as opposed to just a brand-building disengaged from business technique.

In this day and age, market position has never been more provisional. Achievement is regularly a passing high taken after by a tumbling fall. We should listen precisely to the business sector and gain from its missteps in a forward-looking manner. We should consistently change, customize, share and enhance ourselves. Our brands must be an operator of consistent shock. The truth of the matter is everything is moving speedier today, making unparalleled weight on brands to be faster, more brilliant, leaner, more responsive and ready to improve all the more rapidly.

A basic component moderating energy is frequently a need to ensure and vet a consecrated technique. Vital precision regularly trumps the requirement for the brands to react to roll out client improvement their necessities. This failure to change lies at the heart of buyer discontent with such a variety of stagnant and unsurprising brands.

In summary, if you are developing a creative brief to include the element of a Quality Experience, here are 7 milestones that you will want to utilize:

- Integrate throughout marketing facets and review all options to create a strong marketing mix

- Think broadly, yet create personalized connectivity

- Test ideas small, then expand

- Stay consistent with your core brand to maintain authenticity

Measure success on how memorable the experience is to the audience. Set quantitative goals through defined agreement with management. Push the boundaries of what the market tells you to create to produce extraordinary experiences.

PART III:

APPLICATIONS

"[Purveyors of new technologies] must create value by defining a place for the technology; a place for people to put their needs and desires into; a recognizable place where consumers, governments, and investors want to go."

Charles Bazerman,

The Languages of Edison's Light

Congratulations!

If you've gotten this far, you should be accumulating a good deal of knowledge about branding. Let's recap where we have been, and then move right into this third and final section of ForwardFast.

In section one, I covered the essentials of brand innovation. I looked at branding from a value-added perspective, examining exactly how branding can impact your company's bottom line. Next, I analyzed the distinction between "Play" and ForwardFast. I discovered that "Play" side of branding uses tried-and-true techniques, but that ForwardFast ups the ante and utilizes 5-D branding. Then I looked at the applications of brand innovation – what branding means for health, science, and technology companies. After that I explored the obstacles to acceleration that are specific to health, science, and technology and to small branding companies. Specifically, this dealt with the dynamics of team management. Finally, I showed you some of the impacts of innovation on customer expectations and the accentuation of differences.

In section two, I ran you through the six main parts of the ForwardFast tool. Likeability is about brand identity traits – the parts of your brand that are not directly connected to your product. The logo is all about the visual brand identity and how the name, shape, sound, and feel of your brand impacts brand value. Quality Offering is the need to provide a product of quality – and how every aspect of your brand needs to feed into that quality. Associations are the memory links between your brand and other feelings, characters, and services.

Attitude is the presentation of personality to your audience and how your audience perceives your brand. And Quality Experience is the overall experiential identity of your brand – the entire package of what your customers get, from logo, to marketing, to purchase, to usage.

In the last section, I will share with you a series of applications and templates that illustrate branding in action. Each is a simple one-page description, plus a schematic that you can apply ForwardFast branding elements to your own brand in the respective application. For each, you can fill in the model with your own insights. This is the kind of practice that will help lock in the branding principles.

Application 1 - Corporate Brand

Corporate branding is different from product branding and is an important aspect to the overall branding effort. The corporate brand creates interest that leads to preference for all the product offerings of the company. The corporate brand also serves as an umbrella of ownership for products and establishes a level of customer service at a central level.

One illustration of this is my work with Baxter and its "Cellular Therapies for Cardiovascular Disease."

My team took a different approach to draw attention to the corporation as an emerging leader in cellular therapies and also to differentiate its research from the work of other companies. The client exhibited at meetings dominated by megabrands and needed its early-phase research of stem cell therapy to get noticed. The team's creative solution included staging events to create buzz at the American Heart Association Scientific Sessions, while building a database for future communication. We used expert speakers during an educational symposium as well as a dynamic clinical presentation.

As a result, we beat the conference attendance goal by five times, collected 800 names in the database, and made connections with major clinical investigators.

Application 1 - Corporate Brand

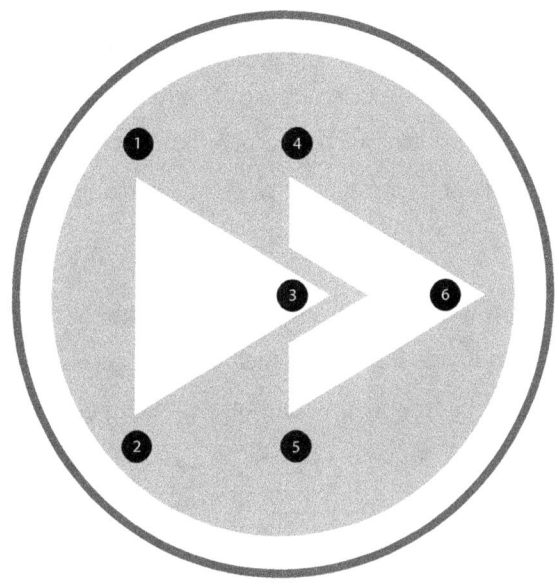

1. Likeability

2. Logo/Identity

3. Quality Offering

4. Attitude

5. Associations

6. Quality Experience

Application 2 - R&D and Manufacturing Process

For R&D, the primary interests are specific and proprietary methods that science and technology companies use to develop their products. The goal is to leverage these processes by branding them. By showing you are on the cutting edge of creativity in your field, you are connecting yourself to value and quality.

This was the case with my team's campaign for Privigen. Because of the stabilizer proline, Privigen contains low levels of dimers, fragments, and aggregates. It does not contain sugar or preservatives, and contains only trace amounts of sodium. The safety of Privigen was achieved by employing a combination of several advanced purification and pathogen inactivation/removal technologies. There had never been a confirmed reported case of pathogen transmission with Privigen.

The R&D work ultimately resulted in Privigen as a ready-to-use 10% liquid IgG preparation, requiring no reconstitution. Unlike glycine-stabilized IVIg products that are approved for room temperature storage for 6 or 24 months, Privigen has been shown to maintain efficacy and stability at room temperature for up to 36 months. The benefit of room temperature stability to the hospital pharmacist is that it eliminates the need for special refrigerated storage facilities, and importantly, allows immediate infusion without the need to warm the solution to room temperature prior to administration.

The foundation of R&D branding became a key reason Privigen became the number one IVIg used in US hospitals.

Application 2 - R&D and Manufacturing Process

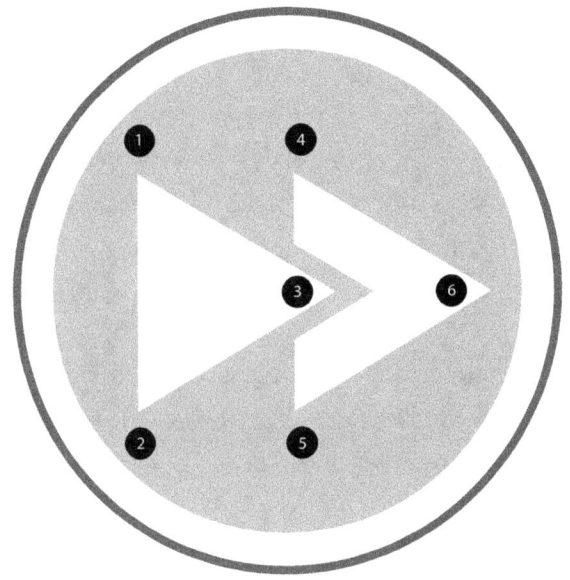

1. Likeability

2. Logo/Identity

3. Quality Offering

4. Attitude

5. Associations

6. Quality Experience

Application 3 - New Product Introduction

One of the hallmarks of a new product brand is that you only have one chance to launch right. You've heard the one about first impressions?

For naming, you can begin with the classic hallmarks: make the name easy to pronounce and write; make it easy to remember; make it something positive. Also, you only have 6 months to claim something is new. You should say it while you can.

The word "launch" has always been instructive for me through the dozens of new product launches I've worked on. That's why a rocket metaphor helps summarize the key considerations:

- Strategic mapping

- Pre-launch prep

- Maximum launch lift

- Post-launch booster

- Real-time guidance systems

- Long-range vision

Application 3 - New Product Introduction

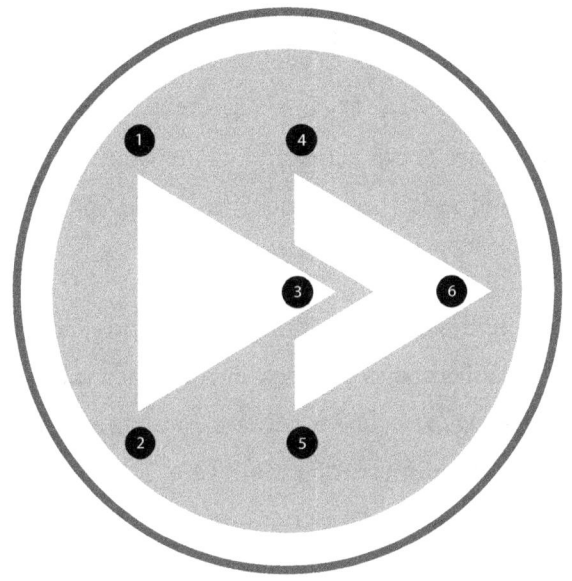

1. Likeability

2. Logo/Identity

3. Quality Offering

4. Attitude

5. Associations

6. Quality Experience

Application 4 - Product Line Extensions

Line extensions are capitalizations on brand identity and equity. The goal is to invest some of your capital to extend your brand's value.

David Cort and Mark Loch of McKinsey and Company wrote that line extensions are about capturing value. Brand leverage is using intangible assets and special techniques to extend the worth of those line extensions.

Branding professor and consultant David Aaker maintains there are potential advantages of extensions (visibility, experience, and reach). There is prestige attached to a brand, and current customers are likely to recognize and respect the brand. One challenge is to reap the benefits of an existing product without over-extending the core essence of the brand.

Application 4 - Product Line Extensions

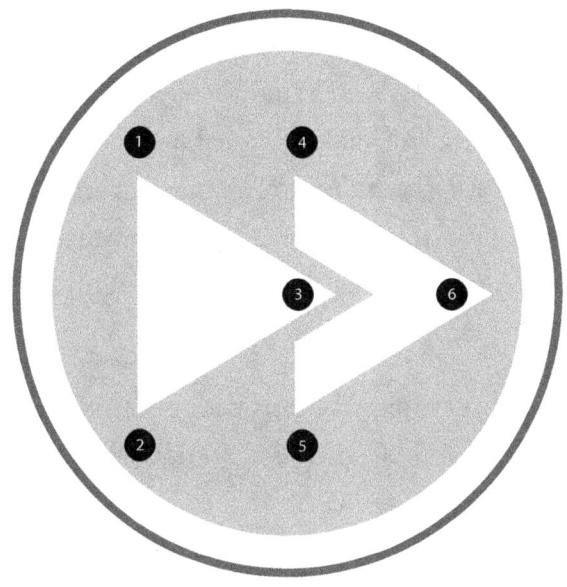

1. Likeability

2. Logo/Identity

3. Quality Offering

4. Attitude

5. Associations

6. Quality Experience

Application 5 - Interactive and Digital Branding

Before the ink is dry on this page, new ideas will emerge in digital branding. This area is constantly evolving but it is still a long way from delivering the full value of digital branding. The problem is that too many ads use cheap tricks or gimmicks, or worse, intrusive pop-ups that disrupt rather than fit into the audience's world. Your goal for digital branding should be to move toward experience and associations.

When working on digital efforts with my client Total Sleep, we started with web design for its sleep diagnostics services and locations. To direct brand messages to three distinct customers, my team created sections for consumers, health professionals, and investors. Later, the client made a major addition of an online store of sleep apnea products.

In each phase, an over-arching creative brief guides digital branding efforts:

- Engaging

- Entertaining

- Connecting

- Open

- Useful

- Easy

Application 5 - Interactive and Digital Branding

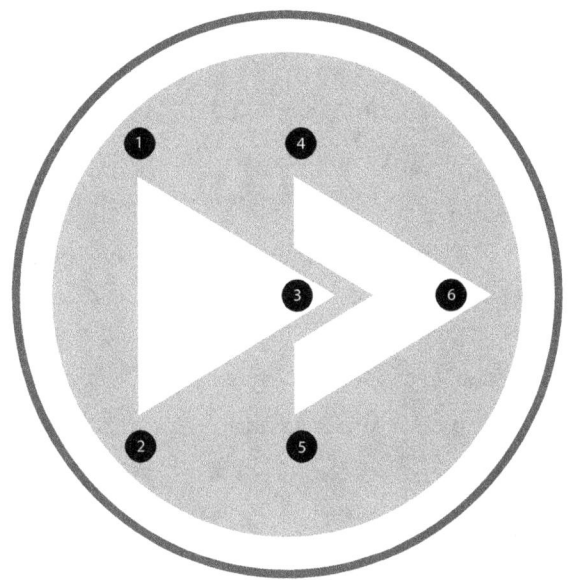

1. Likeability

2. Logo/Identity

3. Quality Offering

4. Attitude

5. Associations

6. Quality Experience

Application 6 – Services Branding

Services are all about quality offering. Branding a service is a worthwhile undertaking.

For example, I had a professional medical association as a client, so its entire line of "products" are actually services. My team branded its Quality Management services as "QMEd" modules that provided clear guidance with the tasks and requirements that laboratories find most difficult to implement.

Another case study is the Berinert Expert Network (B.E.N®), a comprehensive assistance resource center for healthcare providers and their patients who depend on Berinert. Working with the client, my team helped design and brand B.E.N. to takes the hassle out of HAE therapy by assisting a patient in starting Berinert therapy, working through insurance questions and issues, connecting with the HAE community, and enrolling in other support programs.

Application 6 – Services Branding

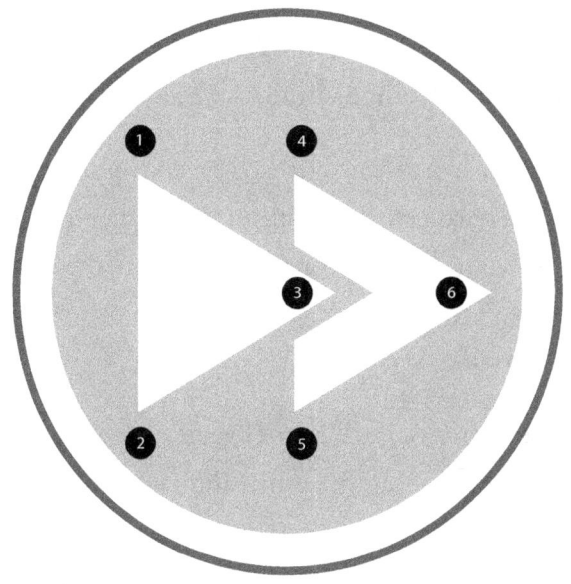

1. Likeability

2. Logo/Identity

3. Quality Offering

4. Attitude

5. Associations

6. Quality Experience

Application 7 - Clinical Trial and Scientific Nomenclature

The current trend for clinical-trial branding is to make the name connote the benefits or method of the trial itself.

For example, in a recent bleeding-reversal-product trial, where four factors were balanced by a single agent, the trial was named 4Balance. The 4Balance trial purpose is to evaluate the efficacy, safety, and tolerance of a PCC compared with plasma in patients who require immediate correction of INR.

In another case, AstraZeneca created an entire suite of trials based on a space theme – aptly named the Galaxy Program. This is a comprehensive, long-term, evolving, and global research initiative. Each trial in the program is named based on a space-related term and the entire program falls under a single branding design umbrella, complete with a logo template that allows for an individual logo for each trial.

A major program of cancer clinical trials my team helped brand is SURPASS. The name SURPASS describes how the pharma sponsor is going beyond available treatments in its pursuit of controlling cancer recurrence and improving survival. It offers patients and investigators renewed hope. When it began, the SURPASS Program consisted of two groups of clinical trials: VOYAGE and EMBARC, each name representing a group of investigative journeys for the treatment of bladder cancer using distinct molecules.

Application 7 - Clinical Trial and Scientific Nomenclature

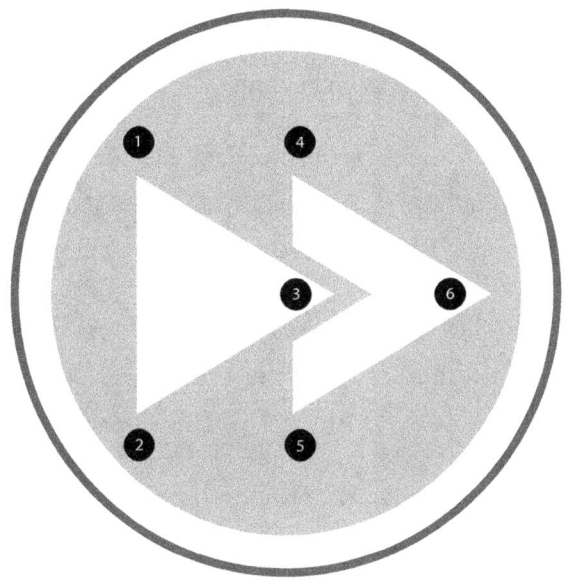

1. Likeability

2. Logo/Identity

3. Quality Offering

4. Attitude

5. Associations

6. Quality Experience

Application 8 - Mode of Action Descriptions

Many pharma brands have successfully created new positions by coining unique actions. Some terms have become so metonymic that you forget they were ever branded claims.

In the launch campaign I worked on for Augmentin, the antibacterial combination of amoxicillin and clavulanate potassium, the term beta-lactam inhibitor was coined.

For the Cozaar launch, its class definition of Angiotensin-II-Antagonist was built right into the brand name and logo.

In branding Prolia, it was important to differentiate the twice-yearly injectable from oral bisphosphonates based on a unique mechanism of action.

Application 8 - Mode of Action Descriptions

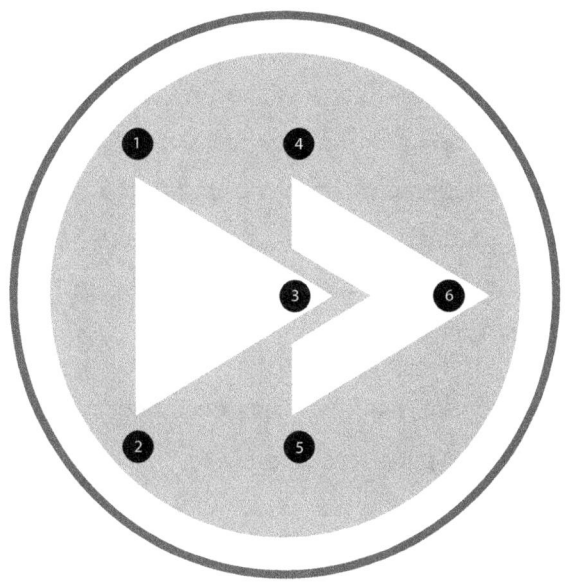

1. Likeability

2. Logo/Identity

3. Quality Offering

4. Attitude

5. Associations

6. Quality Experience

Application 9 - Customer Experience Branding

Focusing on the customer experience turned out to be a great method for branding blood-donation technologies. One product my team branded was a blood-collection system created by the client, and leveraging customer experience lessons from Disney, The Ritz Carlton, and Starbucks. The campaign presented a different donation experience – and it targeted high school blood drives by creating a special social media presence for the product.

In creating your customer experience brand, consider these 7 milestones of quality experience:

1. Integrate

2. Think Broadly

3. Test Ideas

4. Stay Consistent

5. Measure Success

6. Set Quantitative Goals

7. Push the Boundaries

Application 9 - Customer Experience Branding

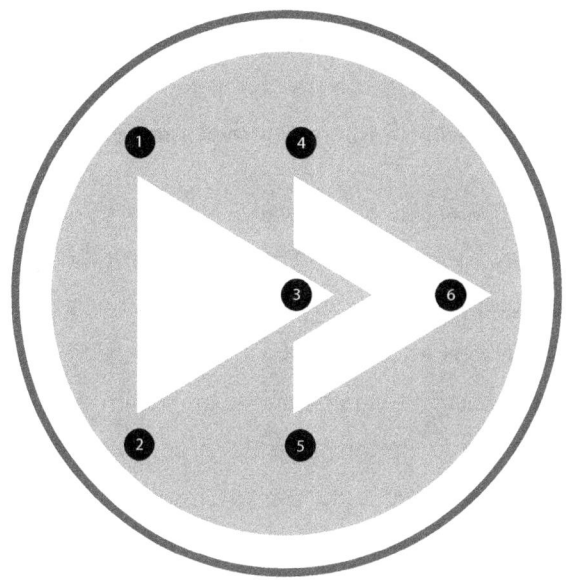

1. Likeability

2. Logo/Identity

3. Quality Offering

4. Attitude

5. Associations

6. Quality Experience

Application 10 - Global Branding

It is beyond cliché to say the world is getting smaller. The world is flat. Your brand should work across borders, cultures, and languages. Many marketers get hung up by focusing on the relatively few differences among markets rather than the overwhelming similarities.

A leading provider of medical catheters for vascular access engaged my team in naming a new PICC biostable product. The advanced technology of the new catheter line promised lower bloodstream infections and decreased thromboses. My team utilized online testing models and a network of global linguistic analysis to identify the best name options. In all, nine potential names were assessed among the target audiences of interventional radiologists, surgeons, critical care physicians, and oncologists, along with infusion nurses who had experience with PICCs.

The preferred name met four key cross-cultural criteria:

- Memorable

- Distinctive

- Likeable

- Positive perceptions

Application 10 - Global Branding

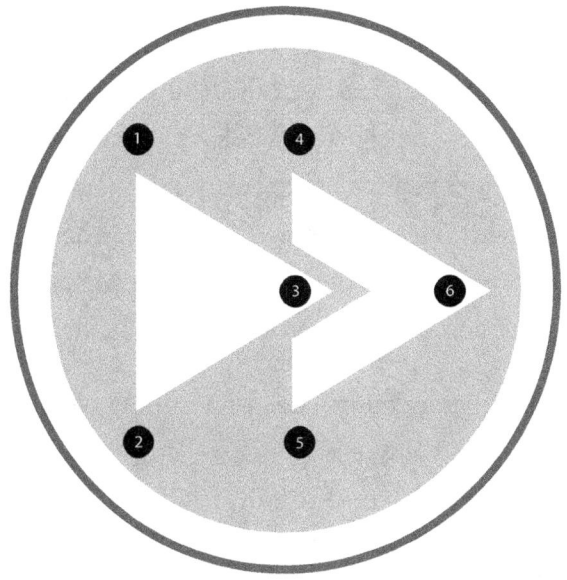

1. Likeability

2. Logo/Identity

3. Quality Offering

4. Attitude

5. Associations

6. Quality Experience

Application 11 - Retail and Environmental Branding

The point of environmental branding is to create a branded retail space. Or in selling health, science, and technology brands, the environment might be a drug store kiosk or a specialty store display. These should be a presentation space that not only makes a potential customer comfortable, but also presents information about your brand in a compact and concise way. In my training workshops, I benchmark several successful brands that can be aspiring. These include:

- **Lego** – giving children the opportunity to play with their toys in shops and, even more so, letting parents experience their children having fun with Lego toys

- **Zara** – creating a sense of anticipation in their clothing shops, driving customers to repeat visits 17 times per year, compared to the 3-4 visits per year for regular stores

- **Build-a-Bear Workshop** – building a brand experience with fun and unforgettable memories in a dramatic, highly interactive theme-park-esque environment. Bright colors, larger-than-life fixtures, and customized music encourage people to stay and interact with the products and the associates.

- **My M&M's Website** – customizing the popular chocolate candies is a great way to add a personal touch to wedding and event favors, add some color to a birthday party, or give as a creative gift.

Application 11 - Retail and Environmental Branding

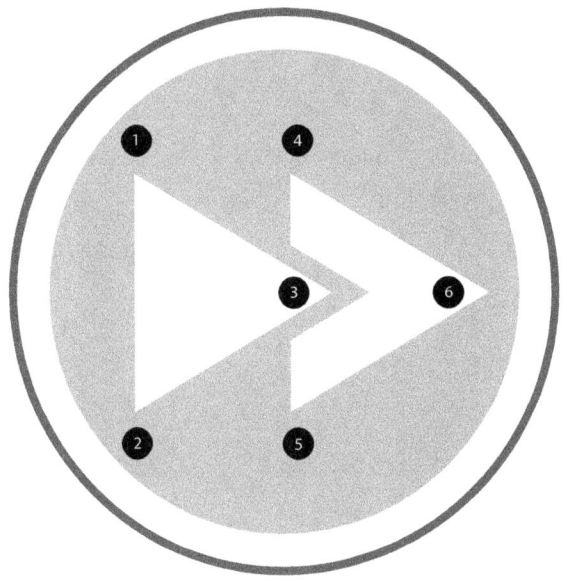

1. Likeability

2. Logo/Identity

3. Quality Offering

4. Attitude

5. Associations

6. Quality Experience

Application 12 - Delivery System

Often with pharmaceuticals, the ingredient or product doesn't change, but the delivery system does. By branding your delivery system, you can capitalize on the inherent innovation of the product.

In my experience, delivery modalities include liposomes, PLGA/Polymers, PEGylation, conjugates, nanoparticles, and cyclodextrins. These could result in improved routes of administration across all categories: oral, IV, IM, SC, inhaled, and topical.

Application 12 - Delivery System

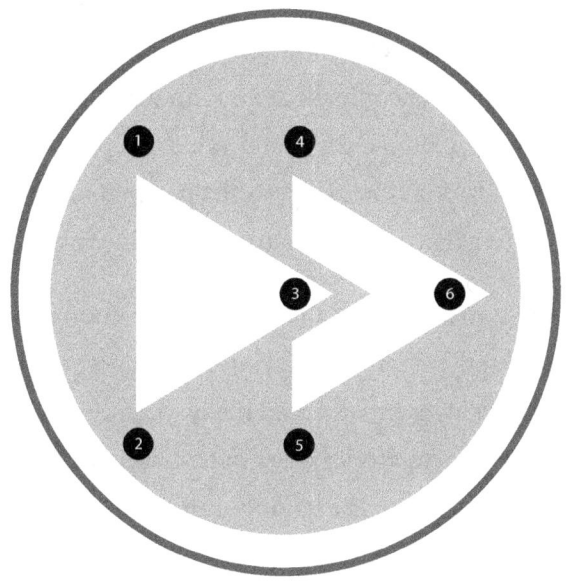

1. Likeability

2. Logo/Identity

3. Quality Offering

4. Attitude

5. Associations

6. Quality Experience

Application 13 - Consumer Research and Insights Analysis

Customer feedback can have a profound impact on branding strategies so this should encompass more than just asking "how are we doing?" For example, imagine the brand value of a pharmacy that calls the customer a day later to check up on the patient and then sends out a mailer a week after that to see how the patient is complying.

I've worked with a tech-enabled marketing automation company called 83bar to brand its communication techniques. 83Bar offers the only system that leverages broad social media reach, targeted profiling, and call center contacts to attract more potential patients to a provider. The group's branding and messaging initiatives were focused on leveraging its difference as a well thought-out, tested and systematic approach to predictable results. It is a proven system in DTC healthcare outreach (including medical treatments, diagnostics, services, and devices), and its software was developed, built, and optimized to reach people quickly – and move to action.

What these efforts have in common are the principles of:

- Recognizing Needs
- Searching for Information
- Evaluating Alternatives
- Making Purchase Decisions
- Confirming Satisfaction
- Considering Repeat Purchase

Application 13 - Consumer Research and Insights Analysis

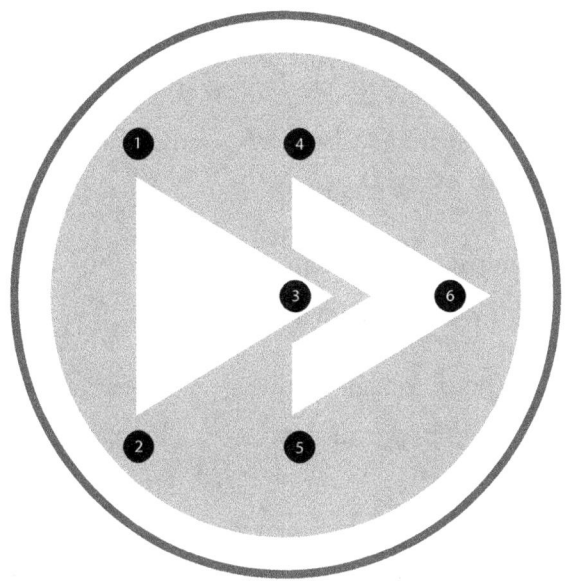

1. Likeability

2. Logo/Identity

3. Quality Offering

4. Attitude

5. Associations

6. Quality Experience

Application 14 - Package and Structural Design

Like the delivery system, packaging design can make or break your brand effort. This goes back to first impressions. Your packaging is just one part of your brand identity but since it is a visual part, you ought to make sure it looks good.

Target changed the packaging for its prescription medications, for example, to improve readability, usage, and compliance.

One of my brand design teams created a packaging system for Urocor Diagnostics that provided all the components necessary for prostate testing and biopsy collection. Each formalin-filled collection vial features a specific bar code for use with the kit. The vial insert spaces were labeled for biopsy locations in the recommended sextant technique. These design elements greatly increased accuracy of the testing.

Key elements of a creative brief for packaging might include:

- Visibility

- Differentiation

- Single Clear Message

- Functionality

- Sustainability

Application 14 - Package and Structural Design

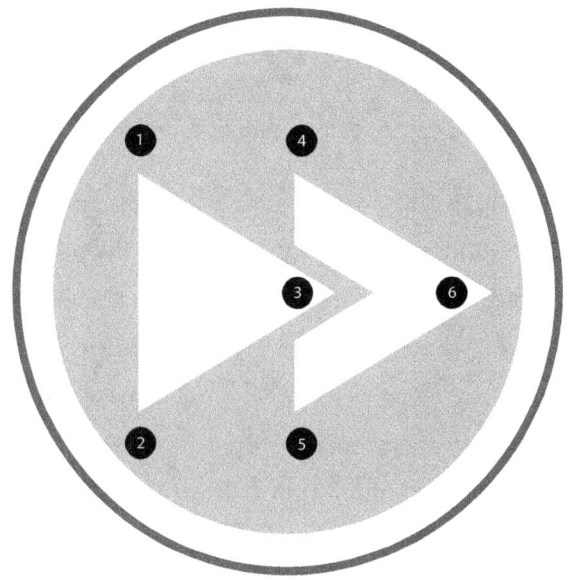

1. Likeability

2. Logo/Identity

3. Quality Offering

4. Attitude

5. Associations

6. Quality Experience

Application 15 - Brand Evangelism

Never underestimate the value of a spokesperson. Often it is enough for a product to be evangelized – if someone we know and respect likes the product, we assume we will like it. Consider the power of endorsements on political campaigns or Oprah's Book Club on book sales.

In medical branding, we recognize that investigators, advisors, and medical professors are vital as "Key Practice Influencers." Therefore, we look to their far-reaching scope of expertise and decision-making in a given clinical area. They are regularly sought out by their colleagues for opinions or advice, they speak at regional or national conferences, they publish articles in major journals, they are usually early adopters of new products, and most of all, they help establish protocols (locally, regionally, and nationally).

Application 15 - Brand Evangelism

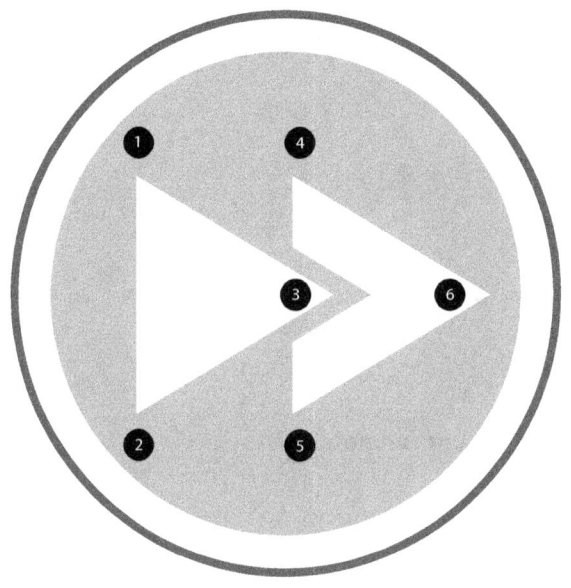

1. Likeability

2. Logo/Identity

3. Quality Offering

4. Attitude

5. Associations

6. Quality Experience

Application 16 - Conventions and Brand Events

Events are a great way to allow potential customers to experience your brand.

Events should follow a C.H.E.M. formula for building chemistry with customers:

- Connect in a relevant way,

- Honestly convey information

- Easily present memorable stories

- Motivate the attendees to take action to advance their decision.

I frequently recommend "meet the patients" events for clients, because it allows real-world interaction and exchange between patients and healthcare professionals.

In another convention setting, for my client Fujirebio Diagnostics, my team created a visual representation of risk stratification the products address. Choosing the road to optimal outcomes by adding an HE4 test to the traditional CA-125 was a way to improve patient monitoring of ovarian cancer. The graphic element illustrates a path with a fork in the road to represent the decision that could be supported by its diagnostic product. The convention exhibit included an interactive kiosk to survey current lab practices, and then create customized lab promotion materials.

Application 16 - Conventions and Brand Events

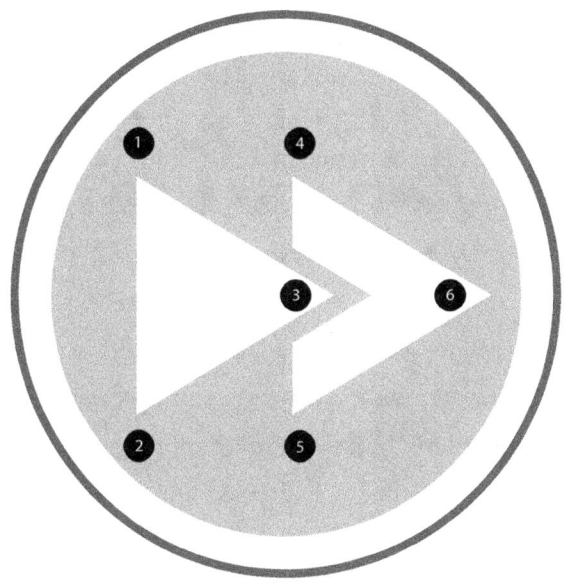

1. Likeability

2. Logo/Identity

3. Quality Offering

4. Attitude

5. Associations

6. Quality Experience

Application 17 - Education Branding

The role of educational platforms for patients and clinicians in healthcare is significant. Therefore, the opportunities for branding should be at the forefront of brand planning.

For one client, the major accrediting body of lab professionals, its primary offering is a line of services I helped brand as Quality Management Education Resources, or "QMEd" modules. These provide clear guidance with the tasks and requirements that laboratories find most difficult to implement. They include educational experiences based on sound instructional principles; examples tailored to medical laboratories; templates to follow in creating a quality management system; online education that is self-paced and affordable; and access to perspectives from medical quality experts.

Application 17 - Education Branding

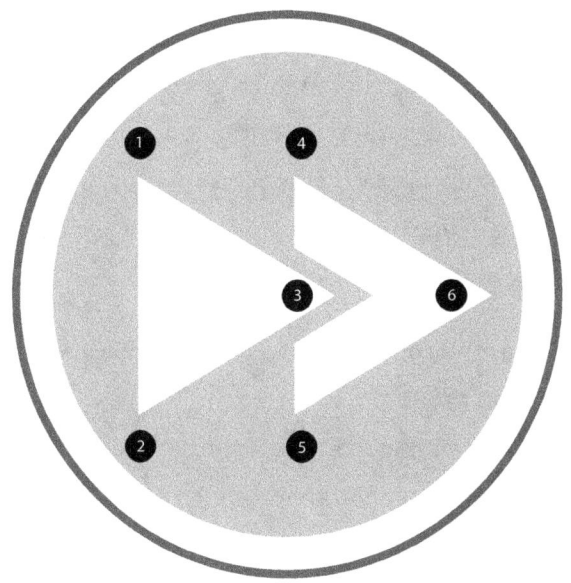

1. Likeability

2. Logo/Identity

3. Quality Offering

4. Attitude

5. Associations

6. Quality Experience

Bibliography & Recommended Reading

Recent research suggests that the books we read changes the way we think. Good stories change our brains for the better. They give the brain something to focus on, which given the number of stimuli vying for your mind's attention, is an important consideration. Good stories also bind minds together, even across centuries. And they teach us the lessons of a lifetime, without requiring us to give our lifetimes to learn important lessons. We can learn from others.

To that end, I've compiled a list of books that have changed the way that I think and as a result, changed me. This list isn't meant to be an end to what you read, but rather, a beginning. Let the books on the list inspire you, change you, and move you forward.

Aaker, David A. *Managing Brand Equity: Capitalizing on the Value of a Brand Name.* New York: The Free Press, 1991.

Adair, John. *The Art of Creative Thinking: How to Be Innovative and Develop Great Ideas.* London: Kogan Page, 2007.

Adamson, Allen P. *BrandSimple: How the Best Brands Keep it Simple and Succeed.* New York: Palgrave MacMillan, 2006.

Bazerman, Charles. *The Languages of Edison's Light.* Cambridge, Massachusetts: The MIT Press, 2002.

Bennis, Warren and Patricia Ward Biederman. *Organizing Genius: The Secret of Creative Collaboration.* New York: Perseus Book, 1997.

Benson, Herbert and William Proctor. *The Breakout Principle: How to Activate the Natural Trigger That Maximizes Creativity, Athletic Performance, Productivity, and Personal Well-Being.* New York: Scribner, 2003.

Blackett, Tom and Rebecca Robins eds. *Brand Medicine: The Role of Branding in the Pharmaceutical Industry.* New York: Palgrave, 2001.

Chaffee, John. *The Thinker's Way: 8 Steps to a Richer Life.* Boston: Little, Brown and Company, 1998.

Christensen, Clayton M. and Michael E. *Raynor. The Innovator's Solution: Creating and Sustaining Successful Growth.* Boston: Harvard Business School, 2003.

Clifton, Rita, John Simmons, and Sameena Ahmad eds. *Brands and Branding.* Princeton, NJ: Bloomberg Press, 2004.

DeBono, Edward. *Six Action Shoes.* New York: Harper Collins, 1992.

DeBono, Edward. *Six Thinking Hats.* Boston: Little, Brown and Company, 1985.

Fog, Klaus, Christian Budtz and Baris Yakaboylu. *Storytelling: Branding in Practice.* Copenhagen, Denmark: Sigma, 2005.

Kelley, Thomas and Jonathan Littman. *The Ten Faces of Innovation: IDEO's Strategies for Defeating the Devil's Advocate and Driving Creativity Throughout Your Organization.* New York: Doubleday, 2005.

John Gerzema and Ed Lebar. *Brand Bubble, the Looming Crisis in Brand Value and How to Avoid It*

Leas, Connie. *The Art of Thank You: Crafting Notes of Gratitude.* Hillsboro, Oregon: Beyond Words Publishing, 2002.

Lencioni, Patrick M. *The Five Dysfunctions of a Team: A Leadership Fable.* San Francisco: Jossey-Bass, 2002.

Lindstrom, Martin and Philip Kotler. *BRAND Sense: Build Powerful Brands through Touch, Taste, Smell, Sight, and Sound.* New York: Free Press, 2005.

Loehr, Jim and Tony Schwartz. *The Power of Full Engagement: Managing Energy, Not Time, is the Key to High Performance and Personal Renewal.* New York: The Free Press, 2003.

MacLennan, Janice. *Brand Planning for the Pharmaceutical Industry.* Aldershot, England: Gower, 2004.

Martin, Patricia. *Rengen: The Rise of the Cultural Consumer - and What It Means to Your Business.* Avon, Massachusetts: Platinum Press, 2007.

Michelli, Joseph A. *The Starbucks Experience: 5 Principles for Turning Ordinary into Extraordinary.* New York: McGraw-Hill, 2007.

Moss, Giles D. *Pharmaceuticals: Where's the Brand Logic? Branding Lessons and Strategy.* New York: Pharmaceutical Products Press, 2007.

Neumeier, Marty. *The Brand Gap: How to Bridge the Distance Between Business Strategy and Design*. Berkeley, CA: Peachpit Press, 2005.

Poscente, Vince. *The Age of Speed: Learning to Thrive in a More-Faster-Now World*. Austin, TX: Bard Press, 2008.

Rath, Tom. *StrengthsFinder 2.0: A New and Upgraded Edition of the Online Test from Gallup's Now, Discover Your Strengths*. New York: Gallup Press, 2007.

Ries, Al and Laura Ries. *The Fall of Advertising and the Rise of PR*. New York: Harper Collins, 2002.

Roam, Dan. *The Back of the Napkin: Solving Problems and Selling Ideas with Pictures*. New York: Penguin Group, 2008.

Roberts, Kevin. *Lovemarks: The Future Beyond Brands*. New York: Powerhouse Books, 2004.

Rosen, Emanuel. *The Anatomy of Buzz: How to Create Word of Mouth Marketing*. New York: Doubleday, 2000.

Simon, Françoise and Philip Kotler. *Building Global Biobrands: Taking Biotechnology to Market*. New York: The Free Press, 2003.

Smith, Shaun and Andy Milligan. *Uncommon Practice: People Who Deliver a Great Brand Experience*. Harlow, UK: Pearson Education Limited, 2002.

Thaler, Linda Kaplan, Robin Koval, and Delia Marshall. *Bang! Getting Your Message Heard in A Noisy World*. New York: Doubleday, 2003.

Twedt, Dik Warren. *How does Brand Awareness-Attitude Affect Marketing Strategy*. Journal of Marketing. 31 October 1967: 64-66.

Zyman, Sergio and Armin Brott. *The End of Advertising as We Know It*. Hoboken, NJ: John Wiley & Sons, 2002.

Acknowledgements

I offer my sincere gratitude to those who have encouraged me to write this book and enabled me to fulfill the dream of publishing it — as a hardback and an e-book.

I've been blessed to receive guidance and support from many "teachers" in my life. From educators and professors to bosses and clients, I have sought to learn from everyone I have worked with, and I appreciate their sharing of knowledge and experience with me. In addition, countless experts, conference leaders, and authors have inspired me (many of whom are listed in the bibliography).

For getting all these ideas out of my head and on to the printed page, I'm indebted to Chris Bodmann, who collaborated with me on the research, manuscript, scheduling, specs, and editing. He demonstrates a passion for branding and communication in pursuit of his own advanced studies, and that makes writing a book like this so worthwhile. I can't say thanks enough for the weekend meetings, multiple drafts, resourcefulness, confidence, loyalty, and good humor.

For the cover design, as well as creating the ForwardFast schematic, I'm grateful to Katie Pendlay. She has been my visual branding partner from the very start of our company and has contributed design thinking to every client's brand success we've accomplished.

My friend and associate, Memet Matt Yazici, helped develop and trademark the term ForwardFast, and has partnered with me in applying the tool literally around the world.

This book is dedicated to my mom, Barbara, and my late father, Jerry, who truly helped me become the "brand" of person I am today. They encouraged my creative talent from the earliest fridge art, they supported my persuasion skills as a student council president and high school debater, and they shaped my business acumen as a young professional newspaper carrier.

I appreciate the design efforts of Colbi+Twiss in refining the ForwardFast schematic to use in a wide range of print and digital applications.

And thanks to my friend and editor, Lori Johnson, who looked at every sentence on every page to suggest ways to improve clarity and accuracy.

Finally, my thanks and love to my wife, Jenny. She not only persuaded me to get started, but also kept me going throughout the process. Most of all, she executed the production of the inside text pages, created and posted the electronic editions, and designed the companion promotion and website. Throughout the ups and downs, she's been my partner in business and in life. And "always a part of me."

About the Author

Mark Stinson has earned the reputation in the medtech industry as a "brand innovator" – an experienced marketer, persuasive writer, dynamic presenter, and skilled facilitator.

His work has included branding, advertising, and marketing strategy for health, science, and technology products in pharmaceuticals, medical devices, diagnostics, research tools, and provider networks.

Mark has worked with clients including:

- Global healthcare companies (Abbott, Baxter, DuPont, Merck KGaA, Pfizer, Takeda)

- Biotech leaders (Amgen, CSL Behring, Gilead, and Salix)

- Hospital products companies (Cardinal Health, Covidien, Fenwal, Hollister, Hospira)

- Drug delivery system developers (Adare, Endo, Kos)

- Medical start-ups (ClearCare, Magsense Nanoparticles, Organ Recovery Systems, Plasticity Brain Centers, Solstice Neurosciences)

- Major university tech transfer departments (Boise State, Tulane, Purdue)

Mark is a frequent speaker, trainer, and facilitator for sales meetings, advisory boards, and strategy workshops. He is the author of two business books, *ForwardFast* and *N-of-8*, plus a contributor to 2 motivational books, *Living in the Now* and *Alone In My Universe*.

He is a recipient of the Brand Leadership Award from the Asia Brand Congress for global marketing efforts. He was included in the PharmaVoice 100 Most Inspiring People in the Life-Sciences Industry.

Mark and his wife, Jenny, have five children and four grandchildren. They live in Boise, Idaho with their golden retriever (who even has his own brand, #bestdogontheplanet)

Speaking and Facilitation Information

Mark Stinson brings more than 30 years of innovation strategy to the medical, scientific, and technology communities. Here are examples of his tools and speaking topics.

StrategicGPS

Mark guides a brand team into a better understanding of how to get from where you are to where you want to be. He also suggests supporting research methodologies to apply metrics to strategy.

C.H.E.M.

Using his proprietary method of customer engagement, groups come away from sessions with a better understanding of how to communicate their brands to the marketplace. These presentations also include case studies and instruction on the best practices in the industry, stretching across key touchpoints of a selling process.

For more information, visit www.Mark-Stinson.com

N-of-8

Limited to only eight participants, these groups draw on the expertise of their disparate members to create bold both changes within an organization and in the marketplace. Mark employs a set of proven facilitation technologies and tools to the table to foster these innovations. The tools he uses accelerate the rate at which groups produce usable ideas for change and capture the steps it takes to get there.

- An ideal group size -- 8 -- with participants who respect each other's expertise

- An optimum timeframe to create productive group interaction

- A set of proven facilitation tools and technologies to accelerate ideas and capture action steps

- Demonstrations of the science of "breakout" idea facilitation through proven exercises

Excerpt from *N-of-8*

A small group of eight people has the power to change the course of an organization – or even an entire market.

This power begins when this group of eight from disparate backgrounds and temperaments come together in a facilitation process I call N-of-8.

I have built my facilitation career on bringing together companies of people and helping them develop brand messages and innovations that resonate with their public. The lessons of effective innovation transcend brand category, market sector, business model, media, and even regulation.

And not just innovation for innovation's sake. When putting together N-of-8 groups, we want to help organizations and businesses in the medical, scientific, and technology communities develop their brand stories, a key component of N-of-8. While stories and innovation may seem unrelated, they actually go hand-in-hand. It could be said that stories are the vehicle through which our innovations travel from the idea stage to the final product.

What is N-of-8?

N-of-8 is a creative brand innovation model that uses the science of "breakout" idea facilitation. By definition, it represents:

An ideal group size -- eight -- with participants who respect each other's expertise

An optimum timeframe to create productive group interaction

A set of proven facilitation tools and technologies to accelerate ideas and capture action steps

In their book The Breakout Principle, William Proctor and Dr. Herbert Benson support this model and this group size. They write

> "More than a numbers game. Each participant recognizes that the others have been chosen not because everyone is the same or naturally compatible, but for the opposite reason -- i.e., because as many participants as possible are quite different from one another and may even be prone to intense disagreements".

There are myriad ways and situations in which you could use N-of-8 groups. I will address these in more detail throughout the book, but here are answers to important questions about N-of-8.

It's Bigger Than Creativity

In these pages, I will shed light on why some people, some teams, and some companies are moving beyond "creativity" and accomplishing such innovative results.

It's because they have challenged their old approaches and have learned that these methods were in fact obstacles to innovation. They have chosen not to simply entertain big ideas, but actually empower groups that can execute their vision.

You have to decide for yourself why you want a model for new ideas. Here are a few goals clients have shared with me:

- Find new avenues to make money

- Expand into new business opportunities

- Modify existing ideas to create a more innovative and powerful idea

- Design new products, services, and processes

- Improve old products, services, and processes

- Develop solutions to complex business problems

- Revitalize stagnant markets

- Learn to view problems as opportunities

- Become more productive

- Be the "idea person" in your organization

- Know where to look for the "breakthrough idea"

- Generate ideas at will

- Become indispensable to your organization

Who Am I, Anyway?

For years, I've traveled across the country and around the world giving talks, facilitating groups, running sales conferences, and moderating focus groups. And I've observed something quite powerful: You could have two teams, sitting side by side, in the exact same room, working on the same problem. One team would instinctively apply these principles and rocket to successful solutions. While the other team realizes very little.

I have worked with creative groups from more than a hundred companies in health, science, and technology. I have written, supervised, and conducted hundreds of surveys, teleconferences, and focus groups for nearly every kind of pharmaceutical, device, instrument, and service imaginable.

At last count, I had worked on more than 75 new product launches in my career. And my consultancy has created or advanced more than 200 brands since 2003. I've outlined the principles of innovation based on these experiences in a logical flow of situation-problem-solution-application.

Then, I offer a series of examples that might best illustrate those principles. This has meant reconstructing case studies (and stories) from both my personal and my company's memory. Finally, I've attempted to document the N-of-8 processes in a meaningful and useful way.

All the while, I reflect on the successes, failures, and learnings from the experience with the N-of-8 tool. You'll learn from brands ranging from Fortune 100 pharma corporations to start-up biotech companies. They represent N-of-8 projects conducted in some 23 countries.

And I'll share insights gained from in-depth interviews with clients, colleagues, moderators, participants, and sponsors of many of these projects.

Notes

Notes

Notes

Notes

Notes

Notes

Notes